D1644131

...other books by John H. Morgan...

NATURALLY GOOD
A Behavioral History of
Moral Development

BEING HUMAN
Perspectives on Meaning and Interpretation

FROM FREUD TO FRANKL
Our Modern Search for Personal Meaning

INTERFACING GEERTZ AND TILLICH
Religion, Society, and Culture

IN SEARCH OF MEANING
From Freud to Teilhard de Chardin

**UNDERSTANDING RELIGION, SOCIETY,
AND CULTURE**
Essays in Honor of Clifford Geertz

Visit Cloverdale Books Online
www.CloverdaleCorp.com

IN THE ABSENCE OF GOD

Religious Humanism
as
Spiritual Journey

with special reference to
Julian Huxley

Cloverdale Books
South Bend

IN THE ABSENCE OF GOD
Religious Humanism as Spiritual Journey
with special reference to Julian Huxley

John H. Morgan

Copyright © 2006 by John H. Morgan
ALL RIGHTS RESERVED

Published by
Cloverdale Books
An Imprint of Cloverdale Corporation
South Bend, Indiana 46601

www.CloverdaleCorp.com

ISBN 1-929569-17-3 (pbk.)
Library of Congress Control Number: 2006929660

ISBN-13: 978-1-929569-17-5

Book Design by Gregory Koehler
Original Cover Image by Chris Donaghue

Printed in the United States of America
on recycled paper

To my family
in hopes that they may embrace
with courage and compassion
their place in the world
without fear.

"For my own part, the sense of spiritual relief
which comes from rejecting the idea of God
as a supernatural being is enormous."

--Sir Julian Huxley
Religion Without Revelation (1957)

TABLE OF CONTENTS

INTRODUCTION 1

CHAPTER ONE
The Bulldog's Grandson:
A Biographical Sketch of Sir Julian Huxley 5

CHAPTER TWO
Exploring the Perimeters:
When Is Religion Not Religion? 19

CHAPTER THREE
Beyond Dualistic Supernaturalism:
The Unity of Scientific Knowledge 35

CHAPTER FOUR
A Godless Religion:
In Pursuit of Evolutionary Humanism 53

CHAPTER FIVE
Religious Humanism:
Exploring a New Possibility 63

CHAPTER SIX
The New Divinity:
In Search of A Post-Biblical Religion 77

CHAPTER SEVEN
   In The Absence Of God:
   The Existentialist Corrective 91

CHAPTER EIGHT
   Ethical Humanism and the New Paradigm:
   How to Spell "Spiritual Relief"
   in a Post-Modern World 113

POSTSCRIPT
   Why Bother? 123

REFERENCES 125

ABOUT THE AUTHOR 129

INTRODUCTION

Our purpose here is to explore the nature of religion as defined and developed in the humanistic tradition wherein there is no biblical concept of God but there is a concept of religion with special reference to Julian Huxley. Of particular interest is the prospects of a "non-theistic spirituality," or, a spirituality "in the absence of God." The *presuppositional apologetics* school of hermeneutics suggests that "all argumentation with presupposition is circular," thus, so long as we define our terms carefully and with intentional presuppositions, we should end up proving ourselves to be right. This is the case with religious fundamentalists, so why shouldn't it be the case with rational scientifically-minded humanists as well? We will explore, then, the possible meaning of the word "religion" when it does not imply a "personal" God and we will also explore the range of definitions of "God" which might allow for a post-biblical religion and a non-biblical god. Why bother?, it might be asked, and that will be another challenge in the book to demonstrate that the use of "religious" language in a "godless" world may or may not make sense.

By beginning with a biographical sketch of Sir Julian Huxley, this will allow for the setting up of the perimeters around the concepts of "religion," "humanism," and "God." We will employ the use of the Princeton anthropologist Clifford Geertz's classic behavioral science definition of religion as it interfaces with Huxley's definition. Then, we will explore Huxley's definition of the "connectedness of all reality" as a euphemism for "God." The intention is to maintain dialogue with the faith-based crowd without losing faith with the scientific and scholarly community.

The point to be made here is that all argumentation with presupposition is circular. So, once we have set up our operational definitions of such terms as "religion," "humanism," and "God" to our own satisfaction, there is no reason why we might not explore, then, the viability of a religion without God, a religion based upon the operations of the universe as understood through scientific inquiry. While resisting the Catholic tendency to "baptize" Huxley by means of Karl Rahner's notion of the "anonymous Christian" or Thomas Aquinas' notion of the "baptism of desire," we might still demonstrate the viability of a religion without revelation. The connectedness of all reality implies a union of all phenomenal reality and in response to this reality, the human community will inevitably encounter fundamental religious experiences such as awe, wonder, and reverence when presented with the profundity of the universal process of evolution. We will argue that awe, wonder, and reverence are not solely the dominion of believers in a transcendent God but an experience intrinsic to the human person when confronted with profoundly moving and emotionally charged realities -- not just a God of miracles and magic, but a universe infused with complexity.

If we can hang on to a sense of transcendence without the biblical baggage, we might be able to move on towards a "religious humanism" which embraces both humanistic values and awe-inspiring realities of an evolving universe. The emphasis will be upon the unitive reality of humanism rather than the dualistic idealism of biblical theism.

JHM
The Farm
Indiana
2006

CHAPTER ONE

The Bulldog's Grandson:
A Biographical Sketch of Sir Julian Huxley

Sir Julian Sorell Huxley (1887-1975) was an English biologist and writer who was educated at Oxford and taught there (1919-1925) after teaching at the Rice Institute (now University) in Houston, Texas (1912-1916). He also held a teaching and research appointment at King's College, London (1925-1935), during which time he was Secretary of the Zoological Society of London (1935-1942) as well as President of the National Union of Scientific Workers (1926-1929). A wider audience beyond the academy will know him as the first Director-General of the United Nations Educational, Scientific, and Cultural Organization (UNESCO). A prolific writer (see appended bibliography of his most popular and noteworthy books) and popularizer of scientific knowledge, he is very well known as the grandson of Thomas Henry Huxley who was the aggressive proponent of evolution and the highly acclaimed "bulldog" for Charles Darwin. Sir Julian Huxley was knighted by Queen Elizabeth II in 1958.

The Huxleys were, for generations, a distinguished English family known far and wide for both their scientific and humanitarian work. Sir Julian's brother was the writer Aldous Huxley of Balliol College, Oxford, and author of many titles including *Brave New World* (1932), a pessimistic vision of utopia in striking contrast with the optimistic fantasies of H. G. Wells. Sir Julian's half brother was, like himself, also a biologist and Nobel Laureate, Andrew Huxley, who was educated at Trinity College, Cambridge, and subsequently became professor of physiology at University College, London. Sir Julian's father, Leonard Huxley, was a distinguished writer and editor during his day but, without question, his grandfather, Thomas Henry Huxley, is the most famous of his immediate relatives.

Since we have chosen to dub Sir Julian Huxley "the Bulldog's grandson," it behooves us to first take a brief look at the bulldog himself in order to more fully understand the life and work of Sir Julian himself for he has said in more than one place that no other influence in his life quite matched that of his famous grandfather. Thomas Henry Huxley (1825-1895), tireless philosophical speculator upon religion and morality as well as being a respected professional biologist in his own right, developed the term, "agnostic," to best describe his position regarding his assessment of the human situation in relation to the verities of life. He qualified early at the Royal College of Surgeons and was elected a fellow of the Royal Society in 1851, soon thereafter receiving the Royal Medal and was made a member of the governing council.

A friend of Herbert Spencer, Thomas was not

converted to scientific evolution until meeting Charles Darwin, but following the 1859 publication of Darwin's now historic *The Origin of Species*, Thomas became the most prolific and vociferous spokesman for Darwin's profound contribution to biological science. The beginning of a long career as the unofficially designated scientific spokesperson for evolutionary science, Huxley first endeared himself with Darwin and his school of thought at a meeting in Oxford of the British Association for the Advancement of Science in 1860 when Thomas' defense of evolution against the inept and uninformed attacks of Bishop Samuel Wilberforce resulted in a victory for science over obscurantism to the delight of the biological community and the chagrin of the religious establishment.

Following a distinguished career as a biologist and journalizing popularizer of scientific knowledge as relates to evolution, towards the end of his life he directed his attention primarily to the topic of orthodox religion. He once wrote that "there is no evidence of the existence of such a being as the God of the theologians (1887)" and followed by saying that "atheism is on purely philosophical grounds untenable..." He explained that rather in its place, the principle of *agnosticism*, which involved the subordination of belief to evidence and reason, was quite defensible. He believed that the moral sense in its origin was institutional and in its development utilitarian. "The cosmic process has no sort of relation to moral ends..." he argued, but "of moral purpose, I

7

see no trace in nature. That is an article of exclusive human manufacture."

Whereas his grandfather commenced the great scientific perpetration of evolution's central role in understanding the universe, Sir Julian took up the cause and moved it forward into the public arena. Born on June 22, 1887, at the home of his famous novelist aunt, Mary Augusta Ward, in London, he actually grew up in the old family estate home in Surrey where he fell profoundly under the influence of his internationally acclaimed grandfather. At the young age of thirteen, he went to Eton College, that most distinguished preparatory institution for Oxford and Cambridge, and here he developed a mature interest in ornithology which won him a scholarship in zoology at Balliol College of Oxford University.

Following study travels in Germany where he developed a lifelong fascination with embryology and protozoa, he returned to England and Oxford, graduating with a first class honors degree. The Naples Marine Biological Station provided him with a research venue funded by the Naples Scholarship and this was followed by a return to Oxford for a lecture post in 1910. He taught the following year at a new institution in Texas, Rice Institute (later University) but returned home during the War to assist the British government in intelligence work, first at GCHQ and then in northern Italy. After the War, he received a fellowship to New College, Oxford, and then moved to King's College London as Professor of Zoology. He finally left academic teaching altogether to work with H. G. Wells in the writing of the monumental *The Science of Life*. This popular text contributed substantially in the spread of the understanding of evolution within the general reading public, particularly in the teaching of biology in the school curriculum. Huxley, as well as Wells, believed that the study of evolution would greatly contribute to the understanding and appreciation of our own nature and human behavior generally.

Sir Julian never again returned to fulltime academic teaching but was, in 1935, appointed Secretary to the Zoological Society of London where he oversaw the running of the London Zoo and the Whipsnade Park. When he finally left the Zoological Society, he dedicated the remainder of his long life to the popularization of scientific knowledge and its impact upon political issues and public policy. He was then and still is today recognized as one of the most important spokespersons for the modern evolutionary synthesis. During the 1930s, he traveled for the government extensively throughout Africa where he developed a concern for and outspoken posture regarding education and conservation throughout the Third World and thereby became immersed in the creation of the United Nations Educational, Scientific and Cultural Organization to be its first Director-General in 1946. After a long and scientifically productive and happy family life, he died on 14 February 1975 in London.

Our interest here, rather than a biographical study of his life and work, is to explore the impact

9

of his thought upon modern day humanism and its relationship to traditional religious thought. Huxley became early, owing to the influence of his grandfather and the family ethos, interested in the critique of religion from a scientific perspective. He was a close associate of the British rationalist and humanist movements and was an Honorary Associate of the Rationalist Press Association from 1927 until his death in 1975. He was actively involved in the formation of the British Humanist Association and in l963 became its first President. He was also the first President of the International Humanist and Ethical Union in the United Kingdom and before the 1965 national conference, he spoke of the need for "a religiously and socially effective system of humanism." Huxley truly believed that humanism could serve as a "replacement religion," a religion "without divine intervention or supernatural revelation." In a famous treatise, he wrote: "What the sciences discover about the natural world and about the origins, nature and destiny of man is the truth for religion. There is no other kind of valid knowledge. This natural knowledge, organized and applied to human fulfillment, is the basis of the new and permanent religion," ending the treatise with the optimistic concept of "Transhumanism," i.e., "man remaining man, but transcending himself by realizing new possibilities of and for his human nature." In 1961, he gathered around him the best twenty-five minds in the world of science and humanism and produced a major address on this general theme, entitled, *The Humanist Frame,* in which he concluded that "the increase of knowledge is driving us towards the radically new type of idea-system which I have called Evolutionary Humanism ... Humanism is seminal. We must learn what it means, then disseminate Humanist ideas, and finally inject them where possible into practical affairs as a guiding framework for policy and action." No true insight into the meaning and nature of evolution and its impact upon human understanding is worth the effort without the further aggressive application of that understanding to public policy.

Huxley wrote several major works in the continuing tradition and influence of his grandfather in the field of rationalism and humanism, including his three most internationally acclaimed books entitled, *Religion Without Revelation* (1927), *The Uniqueness of Man* (1941), and *The Humanist Frame* (1962). His cryptic observations about modern western thought dismisses traditional, historical, and non-western notions of supernatural forces operative in the universe to which we hold irrationally but tenaciously. Huxley said in his little classic, *Religion Without Revelation:* " We are used to discounting the river-gods and dryads of the Greeks as poetical fancies, and even the chief figures in the classical Pantheon -- Venus, Minerva, Mars, and the rest -- as allegories. But, forgetting that they once carried as much sanctity as our saints and divinities, we refrain from applying the same reasoning to our own objects of worship." In his once famous but now mostly forgotten Conway Memorial lecture, he said:

> The solution ... would seem to lie in dismantling the theistic edifice, which will no longer bear the weight of the universe as enlarged by recent science, and attempting to find new outlets for the religious spirit. God, in any but a purely philosophical -- and one is almost tempted to say Pickwickian -- sense, turns out to be a product of the human mind. As an independent or unitary being active in the affairs of the universe, he does not exist. (*Science, Religion and Human Nature*, 1930).

Huxley's concern centered upon the certitude which commonly characterizes the religious position with respect to reality, an absolutism which defies rational defense or explanation. "Any belief in supernatural creators, rulers, or influencers of natural or human process," he explains, "introduces an irreparable split into the universe, and prevents us from grasping its real unity." This duality introduced and perpetrated by a spirituality of matter and spirit, characterizes the religious worldview which then fosters a mindset of dualism which divides reality. Huxley's interest was based upon biological science and evolutionary understanding of the emergence of the world such that monism, a unitive reality, rather than duality, is the basis of all reality. "Any belief in Absolutes, whether the absolute validity of moral commandments, of authority of revelation, of inner certitudes, or of divine inspiration, erects a formidable barrier against progress and the responsibility of improvement, moral, rational, and religious."

It can be argued that Huxley was a far more insightful and forward looking thinker than is generally recognized these days even, sad to say, among humanists themselves. Though humanism has been around since the Enlightenment in some form or another, Huxley elevated the humanist's contribution by integrating modern scientific understanding informed by biological evolution. Not alone in this situation, Huxley has too quickly and unfairly been overlooked and forgotten even within communities of scholarship which both owe him much and have yet much to learn from him. A major contributor to the education of the public regarding evolutionary biology and breakthroughs in genetics and the potential contribution to public policy such understanding can have, his long-term legacy to the modern scene has to do with his insightful integration of science and policy. He was, in many respects, a solitary figure in breaking ground regarding such things as the significance of evolutionary theory in physics, engineering, cognitive psychology, and biology. By calling attention to the biological concept of "emergence" within an evolutionary worldview, he pointed to the mutual influence in quantitative change and qualitative transition, leading to such concepts as interactive feedback systems. A pioneer in considering the nature of "cultural and social evolution" within a biological understanding of emergent life systems, Huxley called attention early on to the inevitability of human behavior -- cultural, social, political -- transforming the evolutionary process operative within the ecosystem of the earth.

Huxley's mother, Julia (for whom he was named) was, interestingly enough, one of Lewis Carroll's favorite photograph subjects as a little girl living in Oxford. After her first child died, Julian was born and became a special focus of motherly attention. She founded a school for girls after her marriage to Julian's father and even after her early death at age forty-six, the school continued to thrive. She had a deep sense of religion, he explains in his autobiographical reminiscences, but "not orthodox Christianity, but rather," he says, "a pantheistic trust in the essential goodness of the universe coupled with a sense of wonder." Interestingly enough and in spite of his mother's early influence upon him regarding these sensibilities, it was, he says in his recollections, "my aunt Mary Ward's book, *Robert Elsmere,* that made a deep impression on me, and helped to convert me to what I must call a religious humanism, but without belief in any personal God." Like his grandfather, Julian found the notion of a "revealed religion" literally "incredible," says Ronald Clark in his biography of the Huxleys. Clark quotes Julian as saying that "on the basis of our knowledge of history and comparative religion, I am convinced that the idea of a god as a supernatural but somehow personal being, capable of influencing nature and human life, is an hypothesis which has been set up to account for various awe-inspiring and mysterious phenomena in man's experience which do not seem to have any natural

14

explanation." This notion of religion as an answer to the inexorable quandaries of life we will address in our exploration of the work of Clifford Geertz later in this book.

Huxley became convinced, following the lead of his grandfather but pressing on with the newly emerging insights of advancing biological research, that, "from inanimate matter, through animate matter to fully conscious mind," recites Clark, Huxley anticipates the work of Teilhard de Chardin, for whose now famous book, *The Phenomenon of Man*, Huxley himself wrote the preface in which he sais that "Evolution had continued, with man and his attempts to erect an ethical structure merely one of the steps in an evolving process." This is where Huxley saw the direction for research and the maturing of the post-biblical mind of modern science. Though usually abjuring labels, he did find himself occasionally using the term "evolutionary humanist" as an acceptable self-characterization when called upon to do so. He pushed for modern science to assume responsibility for the future by embracing a "faith in the vast and as yet almost untapped resources of human nature." He said, "I use the word 'Humanist' to mean someone who believes that man is just as much a natural phenomenon as an animal or a plant: that his body, mind and soul were not supernaturally created but are all products of evolution, and that he is not under the control or guidance of any supernatural being or beings, but has to rely on himself and his own powers."

We are, in a Sartrian sense, "condemned to

freedom," and, therefore, through "no merit of our own, have become responsible for the entire future of ourselves and the planet we inhabit..." Therefore, if man is to assume the leadership of the evolutionary process operative within the universe, we must erect an "ethical structure which will help us realize our great potentialities." We cannot count on some outside, supernaturally revealed, source for this help. If help comes, it comes from the human community. It comes from ourselves.

The agenda for Huxley and, he believed, for all responsible scientists, was a unity of knowledge informed by science and systematized by reason. Since the only truly viable universal knowledge is scientific, by which he meant knowledge based upon verified observation or experimentation, it stands to reason that this unitive knowledge can only be fostered by the intentional abandonment of such pseudo-systematizations of knowledge found in myth, magic, and superstitious worldviews developed and perpetrated by religious and ideological institutions. This unity of knowledge based upon sound scientific principles must be established upon six fundamental principles (*adapted from the* Humanists *website*):

> (1) the unity of nature, as opposed to all forms of dualism; (2) all nature as process, to be explained by evolution rather than any static mechanism; (3) evolution as directional, but only in the sense that it generates greater variety, complexity and specificity of organization -- even though this may

often lead into dead-ends; (4) evolutionary advance as defined in terms of the realization of new possibilities in nature; and (5) an evolutionary view of human destiny, with humankind recognized as the chief instrument of further evolution, as against all theological, magical, fatalistic or hedonistic views of destiny.

Huxley's passionate pursuit of a world of united knowledge built upon the solid foundation of evolutionary science mobilized for the further development of our understanding of the universe was ever present in his writings. The term used most often and early in his work was "scientific humanism," a term defined ironically by a biblical phrase. "One sentence, to my mind," he said, really contains them all -- "to have life, and to have it more abundantly." His main contention, throughout his long productive literary life, was that within the worldview of scientific humanism, the human community must be fully and completely responsible for planning and guiding the continuous evolution of the universe. Not relying upon a supernatural power or intervening God, it is within our own capability and accountability, to ourselves and to the world, that we must rely. There is a strong Sartrian sense here of our ultimate freedom to control our destiny.

He had little patience with a childlike yearning for a supernatural being who sees after everything, intervenes helter skelter according to the petitions of persons and the whims of fancy. It is within, not

17

without, the universe that the answer to the meaning and purpose of life is to be found. "I am not merely agnostic on this subject," he explained when speaking of his grandfather's own position regarding a supernatural personal being. "I disbelieve in a personal God in any sense in which the phrase is ordinarily used. ... God is the creation of man." Furthermore, he wrote, "It is impossible for me to believe in God as a person, a ruler...Supernaturalism and revealed religion are dead, because they are meaningless....there is no longer need or room for the supernatural."

CHAPTER TWO

Exploring the Perimeters:
When Is Religion Not Religion?

Before we launch into a full scale investigation of ethical humanism as a substitute for a supernatural religion, I thought it might be helpful to establish sound footing with respect to the definition of "religion" as used in the social and behavioral sciences. As Huxley was so very insistent upon the central role of the human community in the directing of the continuing evolutionary saga of the universe, to look to the study of society and culture through the investigative mechanisms of the behavioral and social sciences seems, therefore, quite fitting. Huxley, trained in the biological sciences, was quite keen to point to and draw from those working in the social sciences as relates to the human condition, and no one in the early twenty-first century can be thought of more highly in this regard than is Professor Clifford Geertz of the Institute for Advanced Studies at Princeton, formerly Distinguished Eastman Professor at Oxford University, Huxley's *alma mater* and teaching

19

venue. Once we have established the basis and perimeters of the concept of "religion" as employed by social scientists, we will revisit Huxley's notion of evolutionary humanism to see if and where there might be a convergence of understanding.

In an attempt to blaze a humanistic path between positivism and functionalism, Geertz has put forth what is increasingly being considered the most useful definition of religion to date in the social sciences. "The view of man as a symbolizing, conceptualizing, meaning-seeking animal," Geertz has pointed out in his essay entitled, "Ethos, World-View and the Analysis of Sacred Symbols," in the *Antioch Review*, winter of 1957-58, "opens a whole new approach to the analysis of religion." While attempting to demonstrate the legitimate perimeters of the social sciences, and especially anthropology, in analyzing religious phenomena, Geertz conscientiously withholds any challenge to the methodological credibility of the history and phenomenology of religions in their pursuit of the "essence of religious experience." This "essence" Geertz, like all self-respecting social scientists, will wisely steer clear of while focusing, rather, upon the behavioral aspects of religious practice.

The following definition has been acclaimed throughout the social scientific community as a most comprehensive endeavor to do justice to behavior without doing violence to the ideology behind behavior. Let us take a closer look. This definition first appeared in an essay by Geertz in 1966 entitled, "Religion as a Cultural System," in an anthology edited by M. Banton under the title, *Anthropological Approaches to the Study of Religion* (London: Tavistock), though it has now been reprinted in countless other places since it has moved into the public domain as a standard stock-in-trade operating definition by all social scientists. "Religion," says Geertz, "is (l) a system of symbols which acts to (2) establish powerful, persuasive, and long lasting moods and motivations in men by (3) formulating conceptions of a general order of existence and (4) clothing these conceptions with such an aura of factuality that (5) the moods and motivations seem uniquely realistic."

The design, obviously, is not to construct a definitive definition which exhausts all dimensions of religious phenomena, but rather to construct a realistic and useable definition with intentional limitations and specificity of scope. Concurring with but not limiting himself to Yinger's definition of religion as a "system of beliefs and practices by means of which a group of people struggles with ultimate problems of human life" (J. Milton Yinger, *The Scientific Study of Religion*, NY: Macmillan, 1970), Geertz suggests that a fundamental characteristic of religion is the address to the "problem of meaning" --- meaning suggesting purpose and direction to life and meaninglessness suggesting chaos and pointless existence. "There are at least three points," says Geertz, "where chaos -- a tumult of events which lack not just interpretation but interpretability -- threatens to break in upon man at the limits of his analytic capacities, at the limits of his powers of endurance,

21

and at the limits of his moral insight. *Bafflement, suffering, and a sense of intractable ethical paradox* are all radical challenges with which any religion, however 'primitive,' which hopes to persist must attempt somehow to cope." Here, of course, we will eventually bring humanism to bear upon this functional definition of religion as a mechanism to respond to the inexorability of life's experiences and challenges.

Without doing violence to the social scientific perspective of Geertz, we can say that religion constitutes an experientially motivated address to the problem of impending chaos in the existential experience of human existence. Furthermore, we can say that beyond, behind, or under religion's capacity to cope with bafflement, suffering, and inextricable ethical paradox lies the *essence of meaning* to which these expressions in quest of existential meaning are enduring witnesses. This implied extension cannot, of course, be pursued in this study, but I have considered them elsewhere ("Religion and Culture as Meaning Systems," in the 1977 October issue of *The Journal of Religion*). Geertz, of course, is not oblivious to this possible extension and logical elaboration of his position, nor is he antipathetic to such an endeavor. "The Problem of meaning in each of its integrating aspects," he continues, "is a matter of affirming, or at least recognizing, the inescapability of *ignorance, pain, and injustice* on the human plane while simultaneously denying that these irrationalities are characteristic of the world as a whole."

Even an elementary acquaintance with the

history of the scientific study of religion is sufficient to establish the qualitative advance Geertz's definition has made, especially as he employs the concept of meaning as an interpretive key. Within his definitional construct, Geertz stands head and shoulders above recent efforts to understand religion by the positivists and functionalists. If Huxley and the humanists are able to produce a religion without God, then here might just be the starting place for our investigation.

"The existence of bafflement, pain and moral paradox -- of the Problem of Meaning," says Geertz, "is one of the things that drive men toward belief in gods, devils, spirits, totemic principles, or the spiritual efficacy of cannibalism, but it is not the basis upon which those beliefs rest, but rather their most important field of application." Here is the touchstone point of beginning for ethical humanism, namely, to recognize that religious expression grows out of religious experience, and it is precisely this "experience" which Huxley and the humanists choose to identify as possible without a supernatural infrastructure. This "drive toward belief" is conveyed through cultural symbols and bespeaks the human quest for meaning, for an existential meaning which challenges chaos and which pursues order. "Whatever else religion may be," Geertz says and the humanists must listen carefully, "it is in part an attempt (of an implicit and directly felt rather than explicit and consciously thought-about sort) to conserve the fund of general meanings in terms of which each individual interprets his experience and organizes his conduct."

Huxley's scientific humanism must be informed by the social scientific understanding of the meaning and nature of religious expression as it relates to cultural expression. Culture and religion, after all, are both symbol-systems which express humankind's quest for meaning. If humanism can step into this caldron and offer an experientially self-validating sense of meaning and purpose without the benefit of an intervening power source external to the phenomenal world, then humanism has a chance at embodying the fundamental ingredients of religion. Any serious convergence of cultural and religious expressions necessarily centers around the experience of meaning, and experience which is multi-dimensional and expressed through symbols. Though culture is historically transmitted as patterns of meaning which are embodied in a complex of symbols, Geertz contends that "meanings can only be 'stored' in symbols," and are not synonymous with the symbols themselves. Positivists attempt to equate "meanings" with "symbols" themselves, while functionalists attempt to equate the social "functions" of meaning-symbols with meanings themselves. Whereas culture and religion are convergent expressions of meaning, anthropology and theology (systematic expressions of religiously motivated ideological constructs) are disciplines addressed to the systematics of meaning, and as noted above, the analysis of meaning will inevitably involve an analysis of the symbol as meaning-bearer.

Religion as studied by anthropologists specifically and social scientists generally involves a two-step operation, according to Geertz. "First," he explains, "an analysis of the system of meanings embodied in the symbols which make up the religion proper, and second, the relating of these systems to social-structural and psychological process." Geertz has consistently demonstrated a receptiveness to the various disciplinary approaches to religious studies, including phenomenology as the study of "religion proper," and has suggested a model for multi-disciplinary complementarity. Here is a point which should capture the attention of the scientific humanists working on the agenda of Huxley as they attempt to demonstrate the possibility of humanism embodying the fundamental ingredients of religion.

Anthropology is an interpretive science, says Geertz, which is engaged in the search for meaning through a systematic analysis of culture, i.e., the study of human meanings embodied in symbols. "The concept of culture I espouse," he continues, and whose utility the essays in his collected works attempt to demonstrate, "is essentially a semiotic one. Analysis is sorting out the structures of significance and determining their ground and import." The concept of culture which Geertz is embracing denotes "an historically transmitted pattern of meanings embodied in symbols, a system of inherited conceptions expressed in symbolic forms by means of which men communicate, perpetuate, and develop their knowledge about and attitudes toward life." Here is the core of Huxley's task and agenda. To create a mechanism which experientially transmits patterns of meanings through the medium of symbols without the benefit of supernatural transcendence will elevate humanism to a religion with all of the essential ingredients. It will foster life and knowledge, based on experience and validated through scientific experimentation, while drawing attention to the human symbols of self-reliance and responsibility to the community and to the world.

If culture is the expression of meaning, and anthropology is the analysis of culture, we can say that the fundamental task of anthropology put succinctly is the systematics of meaning. And this systematic analysis, or systematization of meaning, necessitates an analysis of the socio-cultural structures and processes which constitute the framework of meaning. This systems analysis approach implies interpretation, or more correctly, hermeneutics. A humanistic hermeneutic is possible only if and when humanism can demonstrate the meaning and purpose of life through cultural symbols carrying both knowledge of the world and responsiveness to human emotions. If culture is the experience and expression of meaning (or, rather, the context within which and the socio-historical mechanism whereby meaning is both experienced and expressed), then the function of the concept of meaning necessarily is interpretational, or hermeneutical, and in turn, anthropology constitutes the analytical mechanism for identifying and systematizing meaning such as to serve as an effective interpretation of human culture. In other words, *culture is meaning* and *meaning is hermeneutics.*

An essential quality of the anthropological enterprise is its desire for universal application. The cross-cultural perspective is the *sine qua non* of anthropological method. The same might likewise be said of Huxley's humanism in that it must be universal to be considered true and valuable at all for, in the absence of absolute universality, scientific knowledge is meaningless. The desired benefit in the employment of anthropological method is the facilitation of what Geertz has called "the enlargement of the universe of human discourse." Anthropology's sensitivity to the vast panorama of human experience exemplified in a substantially built up collection of cross-cultural studies plays a vital role in establishing the discipline's capacity to interpret meaning-systems. For, says Geertz, in any anthropological analysis of culture patterns, there is an attempt to observe and understand "the degree to which it is informed." The challenge here to humanism is clear -- it must be universal and it must be understandable. And, by universal understanding we mean a capacity to interpret meaning-systems through the evolutionary scientific grid rather than through the grid of a supernatural reality comprised of a dualistic worldview and an intervening God. Unless humanism can do this, it will fail as a philosophy of life and as a religion in the absence of God.

We are confronted with three alternative responses to the anthropological approach to the analysis of culture and religion: (1) To be impressed with the dynamics of cultural diversity while vigorously pursuing the analysis of various culture forms and contents yet forgoing any philosophical speculation as to the implications of such an impression; (2) to be so impressed with cultural diversity that one concluded that life has no ground and the only absolute is "relativity," or (3) to be informed by cultural diversity as form-and-content expressions of meaning which are understood to be reflections of meaning-reality. The discipline of anthropology, when strictly adhering to its definition as a science for the systematic analysis of socio-cultural phenomena, is bound to the first option --- observation, description, understanding, and interpretation. Nowhere is the discipline forced to adhere either to the second or third options and when it does, it either steps into the circle of positivism (in the second option) or philosophy (in the third option). Likewise with scientific humanism, namely, either it has the capacity to interpret the world within the context of its own reality without reference to transcendence, or it must give up the pursuit of constructing a meaning-system devoid of God.

We can most decidedly discount the second option from this discussion as antipathetic to the integrity of anthropology as a social science. The second option, where tenaciously held to, would result in anthropology's demotion to a mere ideological sect. From the very outset of this discussion, we have understood Geertz to be suggesting that anthropology, defined in terms of the first option, when engaged in a dialogue with philosophy could fruitfully lead to an interfacing of methods suggested in the third option -- a method of religio-cultural analysis. Geertz is clear in his portrayal of the vocation of anthropology appropriate to the point:

> To look at the symbolic dimensions of social action --- art, religion, ideology, science, law, morality, common sense --- is not to turn away from the existential dilemmas of life for some empyrean realm of de-emotionalized forms; it is to plunge into the midst of them. The essential vocation of interpretive anthropology is not to answer our deepest questions, but to make available to us answers that others, guarding other sheep in other valleys, have given and thus to include them in the consultable record of what man has said.

Nowhere has Geertz or Huxley come closer together than on this point of a community of cross-cultural consultation, sharing, and exploration. With Geertz, it focuses upon the data of anthropological research, whereas with Huxley it centers upon the scientific community's persistent, relentless, and uncompromising pursuit of truth through consultative experimentation and exploration. Scientific humanism intends to bring together the entire human effort of consultative knowledge in the quest for scientific understanding, an understanding brought about, not by an intervening God, but by the collaborative effort of a rational community of scholars and scientists.

We need not attempt a resolution here of the age-old philosophical dispute over whether the presence of order is in the world and thus discoverable or whether order is in the mind and thus constructed. The answer to such a problem, though certainly desirable, is not a prerequisite to our observation about humanity being driven to find/create order-system-category. This drive is suggestive of an imperative in human experience --- no society exists without a conception of order in the world or of system in experience. Within religious communities, suggests Geertz, sacred symbols function to synthesize that community's "worldview" (structure of reality -- metaphysics) and its "ethos" (style of life -- values).

The drive to make sense out of experience, to give it or find within it form and order, says Geertz, "is evidently as real and as pressing as the more familiar biological needs." This making "sense out of experience" is what we are calling here the systematics of meaning. It is a challenge and an opportunity, not just for traditional religious systems such as Christianity, Judaism, and Islam, but for scientific humanism as well. The making sense out of experience without reference to a transcendent intervening agent separates humanism from all theological systems of interpretation. It is to humanity, not to God, that humanists must look for the understanding and interpretation of meaning systems. "Men are congenitally compelled," says the sociologist Peter Berger, "to impose a meaningful order upon reality" (*The Sacred Canopy:*

Elements of a Sociological Theory of Religion, NY: Anchor, 1969). Of course, this was said long ago by the pre-Socratics but Berger has brought the agenda of meaning-seeking back into the forefront of social science with his social construction of reality under the influence of Karl Mannheim. "One fundamental human trait which is of crucial importance in understanding man's religious enterprise," Berger says, "is his propensity for order." This drive, if religious, manifests itself more clearly in scientific research than in any other venue and certainly more so than within the confines of a supernatural religious system of magic and superstition.

As we have seen, religion and culture are integrative expressions of meaning. We can further argue that science is the ultimate expression of meaning-seeking activity guided by reason and logic and serving the human community's quest for an enlightened view of the meaning and purpose of the world, if such there be. There is, nevertheless, admittedly more to meaning than just its experientially-based expressions found in religious behavior and cultural artifacts. Humanity has always sought to organize our expressions of meaning and no society has ever been devoid of systematizers, as Paul Radin pointed out years ago. "There can be little doubt," he observed in his little classic, *Primitive Man as Philosophy* (NY: Dover, 1957), "that every group, no matter how small, has, from time immemorial, contained individuals who were constrained by their individual temperaments to occupy themselves with the basic problems of

31

what we customarily term philosophy." As with
philosophy, so with scientific effort, namely, our
unabated effort to understand and interpret the
meaning of life is the paramount human agenda.
"Hence," says Geertz, "any scientific approach to
the study of symbols (anthropology is essentially a
refined science of symbolism) is interpretive in
nature. It is a search for meaning which results in
an explication of the symbol. In short,
anthropological writings are themselves
interpretations, and second and third order ones to
boot."

In our investigation of the possibilities of
interfacing anthropological analysis and religious
behavior, Geertz's definition of anthropology as an
"interpretive science" has given rise to a
characterization of anthropology as the systematic
analysis of *culture as meaning*. It can also be
suggested that, in an attempt to understand
religiously motivated behavior, the human
propensity for order gives rise to an intellectual
interest in the systematic analysis of *religion as
meaning*. The social scientific approach to the study
of religion, as demonstrated in Geertz, is a
systematic analysis of the content and forms of
religious and cultural phenomena. Geertz says
anthropology does not seek to understand the
"basis of belief" but rather "belief's
manifestations," that is, ideology, myth, ritual, and
symbols.

The task of analyzing and systematizing the
"basis of belief" resides squarely in the lap of
theologians and philosophers. If the humanists are

to have their rightful part in this systematization process, they must demonstrate that scientific knowledge can supply a viable "basis of belief" without the encumbering trappings of supernatural intervention in the physical world. If the humanists can show how the basis of belief in the meaning and direction of life can be found within rather than outside phenomenal reality, then the agenda is set. Purveyors of religious faith have contended all along that the only legitimate source and basis of belief is outside this world rather than inside it, is supernatural rather than natural, is external and alien rather than intrinsic and intimate to the universe. For Huxley and most humanists of the modern period, the discovery of DNA and genetics, atomic theory, and the new physics give grounds for hope that religion as a meaning-system can be earth-based rather than heaven-based and intrinsic to the world rather than alien to it. Religion without God rather than because of God is the demonstration called for within the humanist movement. If a meaning-system can be established without dependence upon supernaturalism, then ethical humanism might just rightfully be called a *religion without God* and propose a *religious humanism as spiritual journey.*

Human experience finds expression through the meaning-systems of culture and religion. The analysis of experientially stimulated meaning-expressions and the systematization of this analytic enterprise has occupied our time through these deliberations. That we have defined religion and culture in terms of the category of experience must

33

necessarily inform our definition of anthropology. More precisely, our effort is to nurture an anthropological method which is concentrated upon experiential meaning as the key to understanding both culture and religion. From this we can argue that both religion and culture are meaning systems and meaning is hermeneutics, that is, an interpretational construct. Just as surely as culture is this-worldly yet a meaning-system, religion might likewise be described as a meaning-system based in this world rather than a supernatural world if and when (and only, if and when) the meaning-system which it embraces *resonates experientially* within the human community. It is experiential validation that humanists seek in their presentation of a godless religion, a religion drawing from scientific knowledge which itself fosters and nurtures awe, wonder, and reverence within the human heart.

CHAPTER THREE

Beyond Dualistic Supernaturalism:
The Unity of Scientific Knowledge

From the outset, Huxley and his cadre of colleagues in the humanist tradition have been promoted as the cutting edge of post-Darwinian evolutionary biology. This is, of course, not to say that humanism is coterminous with either Huxley nor 20th century scientific knowledge. Humanism has been around in a variety of forms for centuries, gaining ground of respectability profoundly during the Enlightenment. The philosophical foundations of 20th century humanism fostered by John Dewey, Bertrand Russell, and Julian Huxley recognized the pre-Darwinian schools of ontological materialism and epistemological rationalism as their legitimate precursors. "There are dominant systems of ideas," Huxley explained in his *Essays of a Humanist* (London: Chatto & Windus, 1964), "which guide thought and action during a given period of human history, just as there exist dominant types of organisms during a given period of biological evolution."

This paralleling of ideology and evolution was a common practice of Huxley as he worked to integrate ideas and biology into his overall evolutionary thought. Pat Duffy Hutcheon* has observed that Huxley "felt that in his time, even the humanist outlook was still being defined in terms of the dominant idea system of philosophical dualism, as implied by the division of reality into the 'spiritual' versus the 'material,' or the 'sacred' versus the 'secular'." This, she argues, "was a worldview which forced free thinkers into an axiomatic form of rationalism based on an autonomous, logically structured mind capable of acting upon and observing the material reality from the outside, while at the same time committing them to a materialism that denied the very possibility of such a mind, as well as of the existence and causal potential of non-material phenomena such as values, ideals and cultural norms."

Huxley and those who followed closely his thought and the direction of his work were convinced that dualism, whether supported by humanists or supernaturalists, had been disenfranchised by evolutionary biology which has demonstrated the unity of all reality. The continual maintenance of dualistic constructs is no longer conceivable to the rational mind informed by scientific knowledge since Darwin. The push for a unitive construct of scientific understanding of all reality, the world and all that therein is, came early from Thomas Henry Huxley himself who observed that "materialism and spiritualism are both opposite poles of the same absurdity." Hutcheon calls Huxley's solution an "ontology of evolutionary naturalism," but whereas the grandfather was taken with his own originally constructed concept of "agnosticism," the grandson was eager to employ traditional language for a profoundly anti-dualistic worldview. The language of religion was, for Julian, an attraction and a challenge. That is, how to use the concept of "religion" without allowing it to carry a supernaturalistic cosmology and worldview. Can religion exist as a concept addressing "meaning systems" without being burdened with the superstitious notions of an interventionist deity? Can there be a religion without God?

Like his grandfather, Julian was concerned not only with what is believed in terms of the unity of the universe but also why it is believed. Because of magic and superstition, there is a strong and popular tribalistic notion of a God who intervenes in the workings of the universe and in the affairs of individual persons based upon prayerful appeals and deistic whim. For Julian, the notion of a post-biblical religion was conceivable within the framework of a definition of religion which was not supernatural but natural, not dualistic but unitive, a term applicable to the human quest for meaning in a world characterized by direction and purpose, especially if that direction and purpose were quite decidedly a self-consciously human construct.

The mandate for Julian had been laid down by his grandfather's pronouncement, "Moral responsibility lies in diligently weighing the evidence. We must actively doubt; we have to continually scrutinize all our views, not take them on trust." This, of course, Julian was initially prepared to do as were and are all self-respecting humanists. But Julian wished to go further for *beyond questioning, one wishes to affirm.* Beyond challenging every insight, one wishes to move to a level of affirmation of the presence of morality within the human community, not of divine origin but decidedly of human origin. In my book, *Naturally Good: A Behavioral History of Moral Development* (Cloverdale Books, 2005), I made a case for the gradual emergence of a defense of morality generated from within the human experience and evolutionary process rather than derived from supernatural origins. This was, likewise, Julian Huxley's agenda. There is morality in the world. It is a human construct, it grew out of the inevitabilities of the evolutionary process. Superstitious forms of religion appropriated morality for their own uses, for human manipulation, control, and dominance. With evolutionary biology, we understand now the origins and purpose of moral behavior. It assures survival of the species. It even fosters and nurtures continuance of the human presence in the universe.

Thomas Henry Huxley's agnosticism went only half way, not nearly so far as Julian Huxley wished and intended. The grandfather has said about agnosticism that it is "not a creed, but a method, the essence of which lies in the rigorous application of a single principle ... it is the fundamental axiom of modern science .. Do not pretend that conclusions are certain which are not demonstrated or demonstrable." Certainly, this is a true *modus operandi* for any scientific, rationalist, and humanistic endeavor. Method, not creed, is certainly the character of agnosticism and Julian understood his grandfather quite clearly on this point. But that was just the point Julian wanted to take further, to say something positive, to embrace the universe in one fell swoop of unitary scientific knowledge.

Settling for "not knowing" was not good enough for Julian as a stopping place, though it served well as a beginning place. Hutcheon clearly points out that Thomas Henry "was, in fact, switching the emphasis to the scientific method of inquiry, with all its strengths and limitations, as the sole source of reliable knowledge....and to this day many humanists tend to write off agnostics as people who merely refuse to take a stand on the question of theism." It might be argued, agreeing as we do lest we quibble with Hutcheon, that Thomas Henry had to produce an intellectual position called "agnosticism" before Julian could reach a position called *evolutionary humanism*. That is to say, Thomas Henry's battles, royal as they were, for the fundamentally central methodology of scientific enquiry served as a precursor to Julian's attempts to move beyond merely "not knowing" to "knowing within the universe" rather than "knowing outside the universe" as espoused by supernaturalists. To get from a " supernaturally revealed religion" to a "religion from within the world" was as great a step forward on Julian's part as getting from philosophical rationalism to scientific methodology on the part of Thomas

Henry.

Restructuring the paradigm was precisely Julian Huxley's agenda, agrees Hutcheon. Having been captivated by the scientific work and theoretical implications of his grandfather and those eminent colleagues who surrounded and supported Thomas Henry Huxley's embracing the life's work of Darwin, Julian Huxley was determined to both perpetrate and contribute to that endeavor. Under the general title of "evolutionary humanism," though a small glossary of alternate terms emerged over the years, Huxley commenced his real work only after departing from the academy. There he had earned his spurs as a serious research scientist, but it was in the journalistic world of popular writing that he earned his rightful place in the history of both modern science and of humanistic trends of thought particularly promoted by that hallowed publication of British humanists entitled *The Rationalist* (renamed *The Humanist* in 1957).

Hutcheon has said what many within the scientific community already know but fail to mention, namely, "Huxley was a far more innovative thinker than is generally recognized today, even by humanists." I would think rather that it is still recognized in distinguished circles of thought but, sadly, seldom is the credit verbalized. Virtually nothing was known of solid scientific value about genetics during Thomas Henry's time and with the coming of Julian there was a concomitant advancement, even exponential, in our growing knowledge of genetics as it relates to evolutionary processes. Huxley spoke of and wrote about these advancements but, even though a distinguished biologist, his major and long lasting contributions, says Hutcheon, are in the area of the interrelatedness of science and culture, of biology and psychology, of organic processes and personality. Building upon his grandfather's popularized term "emergence," further advanced and developed by the distinguished sociologists, George Herbert Mead and Charles Horton Cooley, Huxley pressed to demonstrate how the implosion of quantitative change can eventuate into qualitative transformations in biology and human culture as well.

The fascinating field of early human cultural development has profited from the legacy of Huxley's work in symbolic language and the interrelationship between evolving anatomy and cultural sensitivities such as art, music, and language, with special interest in meaning systems expressed in archaic and tribal cosmologies, worldviews, mythologies, and symbols. "The critical point in the evolution of man was the change of state when wholly new properties emerged in evolving life," explains Huxley, "when he acquired the use of verbal concepts and could organize his experience into a common pool" (Huxley, *Evolution in Action*, NY: Mentor Books, 1953). Movement from the savannahs to cave habitation was greatly facilitated by the early skill developed in the manipulation of fire, fire which was needed to clear the caves of carnivores thereby making them safe for human habitation.

By domiciling in the caves, early humans were protected on three sides by cave walls and on the fourth by the fire made big and warm and nurturing in the entrance. From this simple reconfiguration of human interaction, around a fire, music, artistic expression, and language found their cradle of nurture. Here, stories were told and reenacted by music and art, such that language acuity continued to accelerate in consert with the continual acceleration of neurological refinement facilitated by a more nutritious diet. Language was the carrier of these mind-processes, the mechanism for the fostering of ideological finesse, story embellishment, aesthetic expression. And, eventually and inevitably, an emerging history, a composite of stories and music and art all conveyed the dynamics of human experience, on the hunt, in the family, within the context and framework of the community.

Huxley's profound assault upon the old materialism of the nineteenth century, explains Hutcheon, was based upon his deep understanding of the role of evolution in the survival of the universe and of humankind. The "high degree of mental organization" exemplified in early humans' quest for survival simply demonstrated that survival was made possible by the emergence of the corporate experience of mental development -- in language, in art, in music, in socialization skills. These were crucial, indispensable, for human survival because without language and social skills needed for cooporation, there could be no survival. Leisure is the cradle of culture, and culture is the bearer of human survival. And it was the developed skills of fire manipulation which ushered in leisure, its possibility and its reality, as the caves became domiciles and the home fires became the nurture envelope of story and language, of artistic expression (on the cave walls, on the spears and ax handles, on the clothing and personal grooming as demonstrated in the coiffure of the Venus of Willendorf, circa 40,000 BP). The link between ideology and behavior is as profound as the link between language and ideology. Call it "mind" if one wishes or call it ideational cogitations, it does not really matter. The fact is that human intellect, knowledge, and wisdom were birthed on the cave floors and walls around the fires of prehistoric human communities.

One might be inclined to quibble with Hutcheon when she rather enthusiastically says of Huxley that he was "perhaps the first evolutionary theorist to recognize the reality and causal significance of human society and culture," but her heart is in the right place. One can easily recall the profound contribution that Teilhard de Chardin has made to this discussion as it relates to evolutionary theory and socialization of human behavior evidenced in his now world acclaimed *Le Phenomene Humain* (Paris: Editions du Seuil, 1955), a book for which Julian Huxley himself wrote the introduction. The opening paragraph, translated in London in 1958 for the English edition, begins like this:

> *The Phenomenon of Man* is a very remarkable work by a very remarkable

human being. Pere Teilhard de Chardin was at the same time a Jesuit Father and a distinguished paleontologist. In *The Phenomenon of Man* he has effected a threefold synthesis -- of the material and physical world with the world of mind and spirit; of the past with the future; and of variety with unity, the many with the one.

Almost in anticipation of Teilhard de Chardin, Huxley emphasized that in a world become conscious of itself (through the neurological refinement of the human brain), future emergence of the universe will be through the medium of human effort, self-reflectivity, evidenced in the burgeoning of that complex of human behavior called symbolization. It is human culture, now, that will drive the evolutionary machine of the universe. Evolutionary humanism is destined to direct all future cosmic emergings. In his little classic, entitled *Knowledge, Morality and Destiny* (NY: Mentor Books, 1957) and originally published under the much less desirable title of *New Bottles for New Wine*, Huxley saw this matrix of human endeavor, i.e., culture, as profoundly and uniquely the human contribution to the evolving universe. This matrix called culture "enabled life to transcend itself, by making possible a second mechanism for continuity and change in addition to the genetic outfit in the chromosomes. This is man's method of utilizing cumulative experience, which gives him new powers over nature and new and more rapid methods of adjustment to changing situations."

Though wrongfully and, by his critics, unfairly criticized for his early musings regarding the future prospects of modern science rationally addressing the complex issues regarding eugenics, Huxley never believed that the human community, driven by its biologically mandated impetus for survival, would employ genetic engineering to our own demise. Trusting in the rational utility of scientific knowledge, Huxley pled for an intentionality of genetic research designed for not merely survival but improvement of human life. Today, if he had been attended to in the fashion which now science calls out for, we might be moving full speed ahead in stem cell research and all genetically related research agendas. To forbid any form of genetic research for fear that someone somewhere for some less than noble reason might be inclined to misuse such research is a poor argument, indeed, against the effort. Such little confidence in the make-up of the human character, individually and socially, Huxley would condemn out of hand. To use Nazi research practices as an argument against scientific research is no less unreasonable than using obesity as an argument against eating. Only those suffering from the oppression of a supernaturalism which counts on a notion of original sin would have such little confidence in the scientific community's capacity to monitor its own findings. Only those who believe that an outside source of morality, an interventionist deity determined to guide the world in its own image, would so blatantly indict the integrity of human kind. For social policy affecting scientific research to be dominated by those suffering from the "virus of religion," to quote Richard Dawkins of Oxford University, is a travesty in the first degree. For those who suffer under the weight of a tribalism based upon an intervening outside source of ethical behavior, could such a God save human beings from themselves? This sort of pre-modern notion of human origin and human destiny is the seedbed of retrograde anti-scientific research, and America, more than most other cultures, suffers acutely from this form of Puritanistic condemnation of the human spirit.

Carefully working his way between the blatant theistic anthropology of Teilhard de Chardin and the vitalistic cosmology of Henri Bergson and the process thought crowd, Huxley was keen to point out, as indicated by Hutcheon, that the "emergence of self-consciousness solely in terms of the self-transforming nature of evolution" was his intention in employing a rather too easily oversimplified concept of "progress" in the evolutionary scheme of things. Huxley was eager to merge biology and psychology as well as evolutionary processes within nature with emerging processes of human refinement within society. Hutcheon again says that Huxley "claimed that the psycho-social-cultural level of interaction, although different in quality from the inorganic level, has its total source within the latter -- as life differs from non-life, but has evolved solely out of the inorganic substance of the cosmos, with no vital force acting from without the process." No need for God here, says the humanist, as the evolutionary process itself is the driving force towards further complexification leading to increased sophistication of function and purpose of all creation. It is the evolutionary process which drives the universe to higher development, realizing all along that counterproductive developments are inevitable as the universe presses on towards survivalistic adjustments. "To postulate a divine interference with these exchanges of matter and energy at a particular moment in the earth's history," says Huxley, "is both unnecessary and illogical." Why call upon a force external to the universe when intrinsic within the universe the naturalistic principles of emergence are already present?

More so than, in retrospect, might be advisable, Huxley was keen to employ traditional language as much as possible in the explicating of his understanding of scientific knowledge and evolutionary function. The very fact that he wished, in his own way, to hold on to the term "religion" itself is indicative of this passion for the ordinary language of ordinary people. "We need a term for the sum (of these developments) through the whole of evolutionary time, and I prefer to take over a familiar word like progress instead of coining a piece of esoteric jargon." By using the word "progress," he called down upon his head the criticism of both theists and humanists alike, each in their own way protesting about the one-dimensional unilateral sequential notion of progress, a notion Huxley never intended nor implied. No self-respecting biologist of the caliber of Huxley would ever be so naïve. Yet, he continued to bear the burden of simplistic criticism as he struggled to hold on to common language when discussing advancements within a scientific understanding of the universe. "In fact," says Hutcheon, "it was Huxley's evolutionary approach to language, and his consequent preference for using everyday words while wresting them from their dualistic framework and redefining them in monist terms, that is responsible for common misunderstandings of two of his ... concepts: the 'ideal' and the 'spiritual'."

Always true to his agenda of disenfranchising supernaturalistic dualism and tribal theism from the academic discussion of the nature of the universe, Huxley stayed the course in calling for the elevation of scientific knowledge to the forefront of human understanding. "Since the only potentially universal type of knowledge is scientific in the broad sense of resting on verified observation or experiment," he wrote in *Knowledge, Morality, and Destiny,* "it follows that this unity of knowledge will only be attained by the abandonment of non-scientific methods of systematizing experience, such as mythology, superstition, magico-religious and purely intuitional formulations." In the absence of a unified field theory of the universe, the human community is at the mercy of every whim of superstition and interventionist ethic concocted by the magico-mythologically susceptible mind. If knowledge is to be unified in our understanding of the universe, the unification process must be rational and logical and built upon scientifically verifiable insights. Transcendent deity has

48

legitimacy only in the fairy tales of children and the musings of pre-modern elderly long past the rational grasp of nature's reality.

More than most commentators on Huxley's work, Hutcheon has carefully and parsimoniously listed the five fundamental principles of a unified system of scientific knowledge as envisioned by Huxley. I will cite her listing in total:

> These are: (1) the unity of nature, as opposed to all forms of dualism; (2) all nature as process, to be explained by evolution rather than any static mechanism; (3) evolution as directional, but only in the sense that it generates greater variety, complexity and specificity of organization -- even though this may often lead into dead-ends; (4) evolutionary advance as defined in terms of the realization of new possibilities in nature; and (5) an evolutionary view of human destiny, with humankind recognized as the chief instrument of further evolution, as against all theological, magical, fatalistic or hedonistic views of destiny.

Hutcheon here has quite splendidly summarized Huxley's overall agenda for contributing to the furtherance of the world and our place in it. Simple and straightforward, Huxley was determined, even in the face of irrational criticism by those who failed to understand him and often failed even to make the attempt, to press towards the unification of knowledge based upon naturalistic understanding of the evolution of the universe. Opposed to all forms of dualism which separated reality into competing and conflicting halves, sacred and secular, mind and body, heaven and earth, etc., he realized that for humankind to take our place as the leading edge of evolutionary refinement and advancement, we would be forced to leave behind tribalism, superstition, and transcendent deity. What is to happen in this world is brought about by forces within the world, not outside it. Our morality is of a human character and our ethics are man-made.

Furthermore, the fundamental characteristic of nature is process, is evolution, is emergent variation and complexification, and not, as dualistic theism would have us believe, a form of static mechanism operating on an agenda set by a transcendent being. Nature is process, not stasis, and can only survive and transform itself within an evolutionary framework. "Revealed" knowledge, like "revealed" religion, is based on superstition and magic, having no place in a self-actualizing universe of self-reflective consciousness. And, though there will be dead-ends to evolution's exploration of variation, there is direction to the universe, always towards survival, and always towards furthering the dynamics and sophistication of survival towards variety, complexity, and specificity of function. Herein lies the opportunity for new possibilities in nature understood and nurtured by the human capacity for survival and advancement coupled in a universe responsible to both endurance and variation.

*(I am particularly appreciative for the permission granted me by Pat Duffy Hutcheon to explore her essay, "Julian Huxley: From Materialism to Evolutionary Naturalism," as published in *Humanist in Canada, Autumn, 1999,* in this chapter.)*

CHAPTER FOUR

A Godless Religion:
In Pursuit of Evolutionary Humanism*

Facing a burgeoning fundamentalism which America specifically and the West generally were becoming increasingly subjected to, Huxley was determined to confront this retrograde mentality with a counterbalancing scientific worldview. This he intended to do by offering up evolutionary humanism as a modern religion, a religion based on scientific knowledge and intrinsically materialistic rather than other-worldly and spiritualistic. He felt that the rational and informed strata of society would be empowered to implement the findings of scientific research for the betterment of humanity if they were systematically instructed in the implications of evolution. And religion, the driving force within the human community as a meaning-system, could enable that implementation if constructed upon this worldly reality rather than other-worldly spiritualism. Rather than based upon the interventionist God of the religious fundamentalists, rational human beings could base their religion upon a meaning-system derived from evolutionary understanding of the emergent universe. This kind of religion Huxley called a "new idea-system" in his 1961 collection of essays entitled, *The Humanist Frame.*

> This new idea system, whose birth we of the mid-twentieth century are witnessing, I shall simply call *Humanism,* because it can only be based on our understanding of man and his relations with the rest of his environment. It must be focused on man as an organism, though one with unique properties. It must be organized round the facts and ideas of evolution, taking account of the discovery that man is part of a comprehensive evolutionary process, and cannot avoid playing a decisive role in it.

The uniqueness of Huxley's appeal lay not with his emphasis upon the priority of human interests and concerns vis-a-vis other life forms within the non-rational world. The unity of knowledge Huxley saw took for granted as valuable the stratification of life forms. His emphasis, the profound uniqueness of his insight at this juncture in human history and scientific advancement, had to do with his assertion that human consciousness itself was both a manifestation of evolutionary processes and has a rightful place at the head of emergent development within the universe. Humankind is not only an indispensable component of life within the universe, we are the "top most leaf of evolution," we are the universe come to self-awareness. *Humanity is the consciousness of the world.* And, though we are part and parcel of the universe, we bring with us "unique properties," namely, consciousness and self-reflective awareness thereby empowering the universe to think.

In other places, Huxley called this more formally "evolutionary humanism," in an effort to distance his humanism somewhat from the traditionalists' understanding of 19th century humanism which was static and certainly not susceptible to Huxley notion's of the profound impact evolutionary science should have upon our understanding of the nature and destiny of humankind. Even the outspoken proponents of evolution in the previous century, under the leadership of Thomas Henry Huxley, never presumed to integrate Darwinian evolution into the biology classrooms of the university and public schools of England. The risks, it was feared, were too high, both professionally and personally, to press the issue of Darwin's possible impact upon the scientific understanding of human behavior.

A book such as my latest, *Naturally Good: A Behavioral History of Moral Development* (2005), could not have been published or even imagined. Timothy J. Madigan, in an article appearing in 2002 in the *American Humanist*, entitled "Evolutionary Humanism Revisited: The Continuing Relevance of Julian Huxley," went so far as to say that "for a long period of time even such agnostics and humanists as the philosopher Bertrand Russell (1872-1970) shied away from exploring the implications of evolution for the future of the human species, let alone address how

55

it had led to the contemporary members of the species." Understandably, the 19th century humanist within the academy has suffered unfairly for being lumped into a social Darwinism with the likes of Herbert Spencer, the social philosophy long and falsely charged with philosophical inhumanity as related to social policy. Spencer never intended to discount natural human compassion nor did the 19th century humanists intend to disassociate completely from the biological insights of Darwin. But it happened, and the price paid then and now has been great.

Huxley, on the other hand, has re-entered the discussion, fearless of criticism from his own scientific community and daring in his assault upon the religious fundamentalists. Believing that "religion" was in the heart of humanity such that it was intrinsic rather than externally derived, Huxley proposed the outlandish idea of re-defining religion in this-worldly terms, in humanistic and scientific terms devoid of superstition, magic, and the much touted transcendent interventionist God, who is subject to the prayers of the faithful and vengeful to the point of barbarism upon those who refuse to believe. Huxley said a resounding "NO" to such a religion and to such a God. Religion, he believed, could be, since it is most decidedly a human construct, reconstructed using the ingredients of a scientific knowledge of the world and extricated from the shamanic and totemistic superstitions of a pre-rational mind. As a meaning-system and idea-system, it can be based upon a conscious understanding of the workings of the universe, a grasp of the nature and function of evolution itself as the focal point of awe, wonder, and reverence without the necessity of a supernaturalistic intrusion of irrationality. Madigan explains Huxley's rationale this way: "Religions, like other cultural artifacts, are created by humans to answer basic needs....The desire for mystical transcendence is simply the deeply felt thirst for knowledge ... but previous religions had become static, too concerned with preserving dogmas and rituals, and were no longer in tune with the new scientific understanding of evolution that had revolutionized such fields as geology, biology, physics, paleontology, and cosmology."

It was believed by Huxley that the ingredients of religion -- awe, wonder, reverence -- could be found within the world of humanity, therefore, not needing to go outside. Going outside the world is what ancient prehistoric and pre-modern men did in an attempt to answer the mysteries of life -- Where did we come from? Who are we? Where are we going? Why do good things happen to bad people? Why do bad things happen to good people and a thousand other inexorably and intractably difficult questions. With modern science instructed by evolutionary theory, we understand these things more clearly and rationally. The Unknowable is now relegated to the as yet Unknown! As science chips away at our ignorance, the Unknowable continues to shrink. And, explains Herbert Spencer, if there is a God, he seems to be unknowable, and, therefore, outside the realm of human inquiry and human discussion. If there is a

God, he has failed in making himself quite decidedly known to humankind in any consistently clear fashion. And if the sacred books of religion are the books of God, he has also failed in making clear what his message is, but rather has given mixed messages, often at odds with each other, thereby fostering centuries of hostility, hatred, and war. One would think that a God who could create the universe would be somewhat more gifted at making his will rather clearly known. As it is, religious people are left to their own devices in deciphering their own sacred books, all confusing, all contradicting, all illusive in terms of a unified Divine message. Just think of the energy expended among Christians over the past century trying to get together themselves, to say nothing of getting together with other religions. If there is a Divine message, it is indecipherable and, thus, Spencer is right again, it falls outside the Knowable and, thus, does not concern humanity.

With Huxley and those of kindred hearts, the challenge to humanity and our "most glorious opportunity, is to promote the maximum fulfillment of the evolutionary process on this earth; and this includes the fullest realization of our own inherent possibilities." Rather than "letting go and letting God," whatever that might mean to a rational mind awaiting intervention from a transcendent God, why not own the world from whence we have come and take our rightful place of leadership? The consciousness of the universe resides in the human mind and, therefore, a rational mandate would be to use it, not abandon it to a magico-religious outside agitator! The religious mind, at the end of the day, would have us abandon our rightful duty to continue to develop and refine an ethic worthy of the name. Rather than looking to external revelations -- tablets, books, prophets, saints -- look inside ourselves, inside the world processes embodied in evolution. It is easier, we have seen proven time and time again, to read the book of nature, to decipher the DNA code, than to understand the so-called sacred books of God. The nature of the scientific enterprise, experimentation, testing, retesting, new experimentation, etc., leads to understanding where the religious enterprise of textual analysis, interpretation, argumentation, sectarianism, etc., all seem to lead to more hatred, fear, and war.

Huxley explained in his 1964 collection of essays entitled, *Essays of a Humanist*, precisely what he intends by the concept of evolutionary humanism.

> Man is not merely the latest dominant type produced by evolution, but its sole active agent on earth. His destiny is to be responsible for the whole future of the evolutionary process on this planet ... This is the gist and core of Evolutionary Humanism, the new organization of ideas and potential action now emerging from the present revolution of thought, and destined, I prophesy with confidence, to become the dominant idea-system of the new phase of psychosocial evolution.

Regrettably, Huxley's optimistic prediction has not only not come to pass but, alas, a quiet, surprisingly disturbing turn of events has seen the rise of religious fundamentalism in a variety of traditions and with a heat and passion never anticipated. And if the irrationalism of such religious fanatics was not enough, many of them, under the guise of "scientific creationists," have marched upon the scene proclaiming the biblical creation story to be true! At a time in the world of science when we are on the brink of incredibly heartwarming breakthroughs in medical research in this country and abroad, our public schools find themselves being held hostage by the religious fanatics of an interventionist God. It has been suggested that the rational mind is under siege from the primitive-minded religionists to a greater extent than even during the time of Darwin. The denial of evolutionary science today in America -- in schools, in churches, in social policy -- is stifling at every level and in every corner of the country any sustained effort at moving forward with scientific research.

One of the ironies of the "intelligent design" people is the fact that even if one would concede an argument for God from the "intelligent design" point of view, that does not move them any closer to the God of the Bible! The distance from intelligent design to the Christian God is even greater than the distance from agnosticism to theism. For it is too clear to be denied that the intelligent design folks are really interested in "bringing the world to Jesus," and not to the God of the philosopher or engineer, not to God as a Watch Maker but to God as an incarnate being in the person of Jesus of Nazareth. If they would come clean, if they would really and truly be honest with the rest of us, we could at least see where they are really coming from and not hiding under the false umbrella of an intelligent source of the universe. The evolutionary humanists can, quite decidedly, accept the notion of intelligent design by claiming evolution itself as the intelligence embodied in the human mind and the design is the systematic sustaining of creation through evolutionary processes of survival and adaptation. But no, the intelligent designers will not allow human intellect and evolutionary adaptation to answer the intelligent design challenge for they must bring in their doctrine of the fall, original sin, redemption, salvation, eternal abode with God. What baggage for the rational mind to worry with handling!

That Huxley is no prophet is too clearly indicated by Madigan's summation of the failure of humanism to displace religious fanaticism: "The humanist approach has not become dominant, and a scientific exploration and understanding of the universe has come into heavy criticism not only from fundamentalists but also from the so-called 'postmodern' school of thought, which tends to see science as merely another -- and not necessarily superior -- ideology." And, if that were not enough, scientific humanists of the *not too inclined to accommodate religionists orientation*, have found Huxley's thought less than easily palatable. The criticism is not with the idea-system but with the propensity to employ religious nomenclature, viz., sacred, reverence, etc., when it is not necessary (science has its own vocabulary, thank you very much) but also too easily misunderstood to the point of bordering on deceptive. When Huxley uses the word "sacred" he does not imply, as do the theists, a transcendent God but rather a human reverence of mind for the beauty and grandeur of the universe as it has evolved under its own efforts without the aid of an intervening power source called God. Why bother? is the legitimate question of Huxley's own scientific mob who would much prefer to employ the language of science to enhance and embellish a scientific explanation of the universe.

*Timothy J. Madigan's essay in the *American Humanist*, 2002, entitled,
"Evolutionary Humanism Revisited: The Continuing Relevance of Julian Huxley."

CHAPTER FIVE

Religious Humanism:
Exploring a New Possibility

In this discussion, we will explore rather carefully, almost exegetically, Huxley's position with respect both to his anticipated demise of the Christian religion and to the eventual rise, yet to emerge, of a secular religious understanding of the universe, called here a "new religion," or, as I have chosen to call it, a "post-biblical" religion of humanism. "It is certainly a fact," says Huxley, "that Christianity does not, and I would add cannot, satisfy an increasing number of people and it does not and cannot do so because it is a particular brand of religion, which is no longer related or relevant to the facts of existence as revealed by the march of events or the growth of knowledge." Huxley suggests that increasingly the rational mind is having to play tricks on itself to stay in the religious wagon. When, with every passing day, we continue to learn more about the origins of the universe, how it has evolved, how the human mind is developing, all of this scientific advancement in rational explanations of the universe has systematically chipped away at the pre-modern worldview of an ideological system developed in a flat magical world fraught with superstition. In order to maintain any semblance of integrity, the rational mind is being forced to choose between an interventionist notion of an outside power source *called God* or an intrinsic model of emergent life based upon internal processes *called evolution*.

We have already discussed, from a social science perspective, the meaning and nature of religion, its function, its origin, its purpose and direction. Huxley ventured into the discussion himself in an attempt to both scope out the fundamental perimeters of religious purpose and function and then to identify within scientific humanism those same fundamentals. "A Religion," he explains, "is an organ of man in society which helps him to cope with the problems of nature and his destiny -- his place and role in the universe. It always involves the sense of sacredness or mystery and of participation in a continuing enterprise; it is always concerned with the problem of good and evil and with what transcends the individual self and the immediate and present facts of every day." We have already seen the leading anthropologist of the century, Clifford Geertz, defining religion precisely so, pointing out that religion "functions" to assist in explaining the unexplainables of life such as personal tragedy, natural disasters, etc. If by mystery (or "sacredness" which is Huxley's synonym), one means confronting the "unknown" or the "unknowable," then religion need not automatically and unequivocally imply a transcendent power source, a God standing outside the universal creation intervening whimsically or upon petition by those engaged in manipulative prayer vigils. Furthermore, one does not necessarily have to assume that the problem of good and evil is only solved by "revealed" truth through the medium of sacred books, priests, divine revelation, etc. In my book, *Naturally Good: A Behavioral History of Moral Development,* it was demonstrated rather conclusively that moral behavior has evolved directly through the human community's growing consciousness of survival behavior rather than from tables of stone or books rained down from above.

But, in addition to addressing the intractable nature of human experience when faced with the verities of life as well as the profound social and personal issues of right and wrong, good and bad, religion also carries with it a system of thought. Or, more precisely, religion evolves a systematization of experiential reflection upon the encounter with the *mysterium tremendum et fascinans* which, in higher religious systems, is called theology. "A religion," Huxley says, "always has some framework of beliefs, some code of ethics, and some system of expression -- what are usually called a theology, a morality, and a ritual." This systematization of experience leads to a theologizing enterprise usually appropriated by those placed in positions of power related to their capacity to tease out from the experience an "internally logical" explanation for the questions of life. Thus, we see the emergence of the shaman, the priest, the prophet. It has been suggested by some anthropologists that the priesthood, not prostitution, is the oldest profession. Be that as it may, the theological agenda grips the religious community by systematizing the faith experience into a code of morality and a creed of beliefs which then, in turn, become the criteria for judging membership within the community as well as those outside the experience.

Of course, we see already that the fundamental ingredients needed to make a religion are also found within the scientific and humanistic community as well. There is a fundamental encounter with the life experiences within the human community seeking explanation and a concerted effort on the part of the more reflective members of that community to systematize the inquiry into the nature and meaning of the experience in question. This is done with a sense of reverence for the mystery yet to be revealed and those specifically involved in the systematization of the inquiry are held in special regard by the community. Scientists and science function not unlike priests and theology in this process. The difference, the profoundly fundamental difference, is that whereas the scientific community will only accept rational inquiry and deduction based upon rigorously enforced rules of investigation, the religious community relies upon the systematizers and interpreters of the faith experience based upon their knowledge of the transcendent power source, the intervening God of the universe, who stands above and outside reason and logic.

All theistic religions, Christianity included and specifically selected here for explication, are supported by this theological framework which centers upon the basic belief "in the supernatural and the existence of a god or gods, supernatural beings endowed with properties of knowing, feeling, and willing akin to those of a human personality." With Christianity, however, this supernatural God, "who at a definite date -- until recently specified as 4004 B.C. by the bishops of the Church -- created the world and humankind in essentially the same form in which we appear today; a creator capable of producing miracles and of influencing natural events, including events in human minds, and conversely of being influenced by man's prayers and responding to them." Up until and in many ways even after Darwin, the Usher, Calmet, and Hales' dating of the moment of creation of the world by the God of the Bible was held as firm and true, and is still held onto with all of its irrationality among many fundamentalist churches even today.

The Christian community, summarizes Huxley in his now famous proposal for a "new religion of humanism," embraces a plethora of beliefs which today's modern scientific mind finds irrational, irresponsible, and demeaning to the integrity of the human person and the human spirit. He gives a splendid little litany of these beliefs such as the notion of a last judgment at an unspecified time in the future at which time the earth will be destroyed, eternal life after death with punishments and rewards based on a notion of salvation through a belief in Jesus of Nazareth as the Son of God, an earthly resurrection of the body, the raising of the dead Jesus, only the Christian belief is true and all others are lost ("No other name under heaven is given among men whereby we must be saved" says the Christian Scriptures), the coming of Jesus on a cloud to judge and condemn or save every person who has ever lived (fetuses constitute a slight problem here but not considered by Christians insurmountable), and so on.

"Christianity," says Huxley, "is dogmatic, dualistic, and essentially geocentric ... based on a vision of reality which sees the universe as static, short-lived, small, and ruled by a supernatural being." Based on the creative and rigorous labors of thousands of scientists -- physicists, chemists, biologists, psychologists, anthropologists, archeologists, historians, and humanists -- this traditionalist religious worldview, says Huxley, "is incommensurable" with it. For the scientific and rational community, "our picture of reality becomes unitary, temporally and spatially of almost inconceivable vastness, dynamic, and constantly transforming itself through the operation of its own inherent properties." No room exists in this worldview for a transcendent intervening power source. This "new religion" has as its worldview a vision based solidly and squarely upon the reality of evolution, an evolutionary process which is intrinsic to every component of its composition.

Rather than try to show how these two views of reality can be related -- they cannot and he is quite explicit about that impossibility -- Huxley attempts to characterize this new view of reality through the employment of religious language redefined in light of evolutionary science. He does this by systematically sketching a picture of this "new vision" of reality. In light of this scientifically informed worldview, "all reality is in a perfectly valid sense one universal process of evolution," he explains. This evolutionary process consists of three components, viz., (1) the inorganic or cosmic, occurring with the physical and chemical interactions which have produced the solar systems and galaxies of the universe over the past six billion years; (2) evidential but rare occurrences of self-reproduction based upon the principles of survival and natural selection producing a myriad of complex variations of increasingly higher organizational forms of life from microscopic organisms to humankind; and (3) in the last stages of evolutionary development during the past one million years or so, within the matrix of this self-reproducing complexification process, neurological acceleration has occurred within the human brain producing consciousness, a self-reflective awareness capable of rational, sequential, logical thought processes grasping and imagining spirals of complexity fraught with potential and utility.

The final stage, that of the emergence of the human mind, is where we are today and where our future lies for tomorrow. The workings of psychosocial evolution, the development of language, art, music, literature, political processes, and domestic socialization have all occurred within the last few thousand years but are, without question, accelerating exponentially in response to the application of the human community's intentionality with respect to survival and improvement. Following on the slow-moving stages of typological development -- from microscopic organisms to vertebrates to fish, amphibians and reptiles, from reptiles to mammals, and finally to *homo sapiens* -- humankind is the crowning apex of this evolutionary process.

Early in our evolution, the human community answered questions regarding the intractable difficulties of life through magic and fantasy, through mythological beings and superstitious fears. As we accelerated in our systematization of this reflection, we produced religious systems designed to foster a meaning-system of symbols, myths, and rituals to calm the fears and appease the troubled mind demanding answers to the riddle of life. Through it all emerged a God made in our own image who would respond to laments for help, protection, and nurture, a God who would punish the disobedient (of the rules articulated and enforced by his priestly representatives) and reward the obedient (those following the rules mandated by the divinely appointed enforcers of the sacred codes which had been received and recorded). "However," Huxley says in concluding this overview, "with the development of human science and learning, this universal or absolute God becomes removed further and further back from phenomena and any control of them. As interpreted by the more desperately *liberal* brands of Christianity today, he appears to the humanist as little more than the smile of a cosmic Cheshire Cat, but one which is irreversibly disappearing."

That is not to say, however, that the basis of this sense of the sacred, this sense of the "divine," is likewise and summarily expunged from the human experience when once we are freed from the magico-superstition of a God of power and might, ruling the universe by whim and fancy as it suits him. On the contrary, this sense of the sacred, what Huxley calls the "stuff of divinity," is intrinsic to the human experience, the experience of awe, wonder, and reverence in the face of the evolutionary creation of the universe. Whereas volcanic eruptions, thunder, hurricanes, sexual reproduction, birth, disease, and death all were once the causes of this awe and wonder in the face of danger, the modern community of scientific understanding knows the nature of these phenomena. Yet, we are still gripped with awe, wonder, and reverence when we encounter the splendidly complex realities of the emerging universe, the discoveries of the solar system, DNA, and radiation. These and many other scientifically discovered realities capture our sense of awe, wonder, and reverence today the way thunder and lightning, volcanic eruptions and floods did our ancestors centuries and millennia ago. In this fashion, the humanist is allowed to speak of the divine, not as as a transcendent reality but an intrinsic reality of the universe itself.

Furthermore, to the extent that we can imagine a "religion of evolutionary humanism," it is a religion not based upon super naturalistic revelation from an external God but rather a revelation that "science and learning have given us about man and the universe." This is revelation, humanly contrived revelation, revelation based upon scientific research and intellectual effort. The revelation of an external super power intervening periodically and erratically in the affairs of humanity has been displaced by a revelation based upon scientific inquiry and research methodology, a human agenda seeking a humanly created mechanism for revelation inside this world, not of another and yet to be encounter hereafter world. For the humanist, there is an unrelenting belief that "man is not alien to nature, but a part of nature.." says Huxley. By moving to the humanist worldview, we move away from archaic dualism to a scientific unity of knowledge. There is nothing excluded in the humanist's world for all things are a result of the evolutionary process and must be accounted for and not dismissed as unworthy, unacceptable, unusable.

And furthermore, the humanist is not only "a product of the universal process of evolution, but capable of affecting the process which has produced him, and of affecting it either for good or ill." It is human destiny, determined by the evolutionary process from the beginning, that we have the capacity to direct our future and the future of the universe. Being the mind of the universe, the thinking envelope of the earth (in the words of Teilhard de Chardin), it lies within us to determine the direction of our future and, as we have already seen in our very short history, this can be for either the uplifting or the tearing down of humanity and the earth. We have the choice, it is our responsibility, the power lives within us, not outside of us. It is internal to the human experience of reality rather than external. There is no "letting go and letting God," for we hold the knowledge of the power source of evolution and must then use it for the survival and advancement of humanity and the world. We are the product of the universal process of evolution and now this product, the human mind, must assert its rightful place of leadership in moving the universe to ever higher realms of complexity and refinement. This leadership will not be, cannot be, by sheer force of power owing to our understanding of the process. Rather, leadership must be in consert with the evolutionary principles of universal emergence. We must partner, we must collaborate, we must cooperate with these principles, using them, directing them, but never abusing them, in the pursuit of an increasing potential for a better life for humanity and the world. It is an ecological system of collaboration rather than a theocentric system of externally derived domination.

A hallmark of this new humanistic religion, a religion based upon this world rather than another, will have the "task of redefining the categories of good and evil in terms of fulfillment and of desirable or undesirable realizations of potentiality, and setting up new targets for its morality to aim at." Since ethics is a human construct, humanity must engage in its codification and organic transformation, always in response to a deepening understanding of the universe and our place in it. No longer left to consult a book of rules, the evolutionary process must become the source consulted when determining the ethical future of human relationships to each other and to the universe. This process, says Huxley, "will assign a high value to the increase of scientifically based knowledge; for it is on knowledge and its applications that anything which can properly be called human advance or progress depends." The fundamental difference between a supernaturalistically driven ethics and that of humanism is that the focus for the latter is on this world, this moment, here and now, and not on the "sweet bye and bye," "the hereafter," or the "life after death," of the traditionalist religions. Boldly and with a determined courage, humanity will embrace its own destiny and that of the world and will own the responsibility, not waiting on a God to come and take us away from it all, but relying upon our rightful place here and the necessity of caring for it and fostering its advancement into higher realms of consciousness.

Huxley's concluding remarks are worth reprinting here for all to hear and enjoy:

> Humanism also differs from all supernaturalist religions in centering its long-term aims not on the next world but on this one. One of its tenets is that this world and the life in it can be improved, and that it is our duty to try to improve it, socially, culturally, and politically. The humanist goal must

therefore be, not Technocracy, nor Theocracy, not the omnipotent and authoritarian State, nor the Welfare State, nor the Consumption Economy, but the fulfillment Society. By this I mean a society organized in such a way as to give the greatest number of people the fullest opportunities of realizing their potentialities -- of achievement and enjoyment, morality and community. It will do so by providing opportunities for education, for adventure and achievement, for cooperating in worthwhile projects, for meditation and withdrawal, for self-development and unselfish action.

*Explicating an essay by Julian Huxley in 1962 issue of *The Humanist* entitled, "The Coming New Religion of Humanism."

CHAPTER SIX

The New Divinity:
In Search of A Post-Biblical Religion*

Julian Huxley's responsorial essay to the Bishop of Woolwich's now famous book, *Honest to God*, is now considered one of the great classics of the humanists' critique of religion generally and Christianity specifically. Our intent here is to unpack several arguments of Huxley without offering yet another running commentary on the whole essay. It is valuable reading in its own right and I only dare here propose to explore components of the essay owing to their relevance to our overall exploration into the notion of a religious humanism, or a "post-biblical religion" as I have occasionally chosen to call it.

The good Bishop's book, at the time, caused a monumental stir within the Christian establishment the likes of which had not been seen in decades, maybe even matching that caused by Darwin's work and the resulting catastrophe with the collapse of the shallow and uninformed contra-arguments of Bishop Wilberforce of Oxford. If Huxley's grandfather laid to rest the fallacious arguments against evolution posted by the good but naïve Bishop of Oxford, then the brave Bishop of Woolwich raised again questions about the nature of God which caused a bestirring of ecclesiastics at the prospects of troubling the easy-going laity. This kind of challenge Huxley could not but applaud and, naturally, being the optimist that he was felt compelled to look more closely at the "Honest to God" debate, as it was then called, which was just getting underway when he wrote his evaluative essay, entitled, "The New Divinity."

Huxley suggests that the Bishop's critique was inevitable owing to the increasing realization among rational people that the old theological paradigm had reached a point of no longer responding to lame and diversionary shoring up attempts by the ecclesiastics entrusted with that "old time religion" of traditional Christianity. The "new knowledge" of modern scientific research is necessarily calling for a "new vision" of who and what humanity is and should become. "This new vision," says Huxley, "is both comprehensive and unitary. It integrates the fantastic diversity of the world into a single framework, the pattern of all-embracing evolutionary process." No longer will the old dualism suffice in a world united through the scientific efforts of evolutionary biologists. There is no viable dualism left in the modern world other than that found to still persist in the troubled minds of pre-modern clerics seeking to stave off the inevitability of modern science. In the absence of a dualistic worldview pitting mind against matter, the supernatural against the natural, this world against that, etc., the replacement to dualism comes in the form of a well developed unity of knowledge, unity of reality, unity of the universe. All reality is "part of one natural process of evolution," says Huxley, and therefore the inevitable demise of a dualistic world perpetrated by traditional theism was destined to collapse. Bishop Robinson's little book is simply the literary obituary to that collapse.

And it is here, on our planet, among our own species, that mind has broken forth from the dark beginnings of organic life. A product of billions of years of evolution, the human mind is the instancing of the earth becoming self-conscious. We are the thinking envelope of the world, as Teilhard de Chardin so poetically put it. And speaking of the human person, Huxley points out, "whether he likes it or not, he is responsible for the whole further evolution of our planet." In words that pleased Huxley immensely, the Bishop suggested that the current image of God -- the supernatural being intervening in the world, who created it and governs it by rules he has established, who visited the world in the person of Jesus of Nazareth, who judges and condemns those who fail to obey his mandates as they are dictated by the sacred text of Christianity and as mediated by the ecclesiastical authorities at any given time -- this God is the God of the believer. "But," says the Bishop, "I suspect that we have reached a point where this mental image of God is also more of a hindrance than a help ... Any image can become an idol, and I believe that Christians must go through the agonizing process in this generation of detaching themselves from this idol." The good Bishop even said that he heartily agreed with Huxley's youthful proclamation recorded in his *Religion Without Revelation:* "The sense of spiritual relief which comes from rejecting the idea of God as a superhuman being is enormous."

79

Still and yet, however, the Bishop clings to the notion of a personal concept of God, for, as he says in quoting Christian scriptures: "Nothing can separate us from the love of God" and ends the argument, sadly and somewhat pathetically, by saying that at the end of the day, "God is ultimate reality ... and ultimate reality must exist." Finally and disappointingly, the Bishop was not able to move outside the dualism of traditional religion, holding ever so tightly to the notion of an ultimate reality standing "outside" of the universe. No unity here, no unity of scientific knowledge which displaces the notion of a transcendent God, a supernatural power source outside the reality of our own experienced world.

Eager to educate those willing to listen and learn from the social and biological sciences about the evolution of the world and the human community within it, Huxley points out the evolutionary phases through which we humans have passed over the last few thousand years --- from fire-manipulating cave dwellers to agriculturalists to early city-dwelling civilizations to, in rapid succession, industrialization, technological revolution, and now evolutionary scientific learning surpassing all previous forms and paradigms of knowledge. And, says Huxley, this evolutionary process bears heavily upon the concomitant evolutionary advances in religious self-understanding -- from totemism and shamanism to tribal religions through polytheism to western monotheism with all of its theological sophistication. Huxley concedes that "religion in some form is a universal function of man in society, the organ for dealing with the problems of destiny, the destiny of individual men and women, of societies and nations, and of the human species as a whole."

Granted its ideological framework, moral codes, rituals and symbols, every religion carries with it a worldview extrapolated from reflections upon communal experiences of the intractable character of life's journey and, in its own way, attempting to offer explanations and even providing self-serving manipulations of the desired outcome. As the history of religions shows so very plainly, however, both moral codes and ritual behavior derive from the "theological" or ideological framework of each religious system. However, when the ideology of the faith fails to keep pace with the "experience" of the community it has evolved to serve, the religious system itself falls into ill repute and demise. This devolution of a religious ideology, owing to its inevitable failure to respond to the growing and changing needs of the community it serves, leads to disillusionment and eventual abandonment. Granted, the continual ritualistic compliance with the tradition continues long after it is no longer able to speak to the conditions of those living within it and under its jurisdiction. At some juncture, the religious system degenerates into mere formalism and ritualism without conveying any of its value as a meaning-system to the community. Time and time again history has demonstrated the demise of religion when it no longer serves the needs of its constituency -- tribal religions, the religions of the Greeks, etc. Huxley summarizes the condition quite poignantly: "Eventually, the old ideas will no longer serve, the old ideological framework can no longer be tinkered up to bear the weight of the facts, and a radical reconstruction becomes necessary, leading eventually to the emergence of a quite new organization of thought and belief, just as the emergence of new types of bodily organization was necessary to achieve biological advance."

This reconstructing of a cosmic paradigm which evolved to serve a purpose but which new understanding has antiquated is not uncommon in the world of scientific research. The movement from a cosmology of a flat earth to a geocentric and then heliocentric worldview is indicative of this sort of evolution. Science, however, unlike religion, is driven by reason and scientific exploration and experimentation which dictate the inevitability of reconstructing the interpretative paradigm. Huxley believes that a reorganization of religious thought is now crucial if it is to survive in any recognizable form. He believes that the movement must be away from a God-centered universe to an evolutionary-centered universe. From the magico-superstitious world of the Paleolithic age involving shamanic ritual and priestly dominion over all things speculative about the meaning and nature of human experience we must move to a meaning-system built upon evolutionary science which addresses through experimentation and exploration the verities of life to which traditionalist religions were addressed in the past but no longer resonate with the facts of modern experience.

"But to come back to Dr. Robinson," says Huxley. "He is surely right in concentrating on the problem of God, rather than on the resurrection or the after-life, for God is Christianity's central hypothesis. But he is surely wrong in making such statements as that 'God is ultimate reality'." This is to identify the problem and then to bail out with a falsehood! The problem with the answer is that the God used in creating the problem, viz., a dualistic universe, is the same God offered as the solution. God is, if I may say so, the illness of which it claims to be the cure! God can't be the cause and the cure simultaneously. God is a human creation and is, therefore, subject to deconstruction. Huxley calls it "semantic cheating," for this God of religious minded people is a supernatural power source outside the universe which is called back into it periodically for purposes of fixing things. This God is not part of the universe, not part of the process, but a fixture extraneous to it for purposes of fixing it when it is broken or needs altering according to the petitions of the communities of faith who believe in it. Bishop Robinson, like other modern theologians, says Huxley, is literally trying to "ride two horses at once." The good Bishop, it seems, wishes to dismiss the popular image of a God characterized by modern thought while still persisting in keeping God who is, nevertheless, a supernatural power and personality.

At the end of the day, Huxley says, really, "today the God hypothesis has ceased to be scientifically tenable, has lost its explanatory value and is becoming an intellectual and moral burden to our thought." In rational and scientific circles, it has become a sheer point of embarrassment. Neither convincing nor comforting, says he, its abandonment often "brings a deep sense of relief." False is the accusation that the abandonment of this interventionist God means the end of social and personal morality. That 19th century notion of "no eternal judgment, no moral behavior" is both naïve and a blatant indictment against the character of the human person. Unless, of course, one really believes that the only motivating force for moral behavior is fear of hell! What must happen, following the abandonment of a personal notion of God and an embracing of the spiritual relief which comes from such abandonment is the realization that we are, then, "condemned to freedom," to use a Sartrian expression. It now rests with us, this development of a moral code, a paradigm of behavior conducive to the stability of society. Gone forever is the belief in a God who created the world and then, because it turned out badly, destroys it only to bring it back to life with the curse of pain, suffering, and death upon it because it turned out wrong in the first place --- thus the origin of labor, birth pain, death, etc.

What we are left with, thankfully, is the raw materials of a meaning-system ready for construction. This meaning-system, i.e., religion if you please, was more than once referred to by Huxley as "divine" by which, he explained, "For want of a better, I use the term *divine*, though this quality of divinity is not truly supernatural but *transnatural* -- it grows out of ordinary nature, but transcends it. The divine is what man finds worthy of adoration, that which compels his awe." The raw materials of human experience include a sense of awe, wonder, and reverence at the complexity and profundity of the universe, of creation, of the evolutionary process. Much of religion, in its earliest forms and in its latest, addresses the need for the human community to explain the intractable and the irrational experiences of life, our encounter with reality in the form of natural disasters, deaths of loved ones, the presence of injustice in the world, etc. In a pre-modern world where scientific explanations of these verities of life were not available, the human community was left to its own devices to provide, to conjure, to concoct explanations. "Divinity," says Huxley, "is the chief raw material out of which gods have been fashioned in a pre-modern world." Now, we know about the evolutionary processes, and still find ourselves in awe and, therefore, continually equipped with the experiential dynamic of a religious encounter without the necessity of a transcendent being, an external power source, for our adoration. It is the earth we adore, it is the universe to which we offer reverence and adoration.

Thus, the appearance of sacred texts, hagiographies, saints, etc., to salve the anxieties of the primitive mind. But now, in a world becoming more understood with every passing day, the scientific community does its work, these verities of life take on a rational aura, and we know why things happen. But awe, wonder, and reverence have not disappeared. It might even be argued that they have become ever more prevalent in modern rational society as we come to know more about the universe through scientific exploration and explanation. The moon has not lost its capacity to elicit awe and wonder at its beauty or its majesty simply because we have gone there. Has the reverence for life been lost now that we understand conception and can observe first hand the birth of a child? Not in my world. Huxley's notion of a "transnatural" divinity, a divinity without God, is based on his conviction that the evolutionary processes operative within the universe are themselves worthy and solicitous of awe and adoration, wonder and reverence. One need not look beyond the heavens, past the clouds, behind the trees, to find a sense of divinity for a sense of the awe-inspiring is generated by the grandeur of the world itself, its life forms, its geological history, its emerging complexities, culminating in the development of a self-consciousness in the mind of humankind. The human mind deserves our reverence rather than an illusive deity.

Huxley disavows any pretext at telling the future. "What precise form these new agencies of religious thought will take it is impossible to say in this period of violent transition. But one can make some general prophecies, viz., the central religious hypothesis will certainly be evolution..." This firmly established principle of evolution has gained this position of prominence owing to the fact that it has been systematically and comprehensively examined according to scientific methodology and has stood the test. There is, of course, no point of arrival, really, even when all is said and done. It is forever and eternally an *on-going process of development*, of emerging new realities. "Thus, the central long-term concern of religion (humanistic rather than supernatural) must be to promote further evolutionary improvement and to realize new possibilities." By setting this as the fundamental agenda of the new divinity, the humanistic religion without God, "this means greater fulfillment by more human individuals and fuller achievement by more human societies."

Evolutionary processes, operative at the microscopic as well as macroscopic level and through time covering billions of years, have brought the universe to this moment, to the moment of the human wherein self-reflective awareness has become a reality. The earth is conscious of itself through the mind of the human person. "Human potentialities constitute the world's greatest resource," says Huxley, lamenting that, "at the moment only a tiny fraction of them are being realized." It is this agenda, the agenda of tapping these great human potentials, that must be the driving force of the new divinity. By developing these resources, developing "a full, deep and rich personality," says Huxley, "the individual ceases to be a mere cog or cipher, and makes his own particular contribution to evolutionary fulfillment. The criticism of the traditional religionists is side-stepped here by claiming the higher ground. It is humankind and the welfare of the earth and its universe which draws our attention in a humanistic religious sense, not a God standing outside and judging the world and its inhabitants. Everything is a participant in the process as there is no duality in the real world. Nature and spirit are one in this new cosmic religion of evolution.

Of course, the ingredients of a meaning-system such as religion will be maintained in the new order because ritual and moral codes are inevitable but will necessarily have to undergo a major transformation, away from the other-worldly fixation to a this-worldly orientation. The working out of these rituals and codes, symbols and storytellings will be part and parcel of the process of the new divinity. So, replacing the traditionalists' self-centered focus upon "eternity," a "heavenly abode in the after awhile," the new order will direct our attention to the evolutionary process itself. Petitionary prayer in a world without a transcendent intervening being is out of order but the formalized process of articulating "aspirations and self-explorations" in an emotional posture of awe, wonder, and reverence will certainly be in order. Meditation and self-examination, says Huxley, will have its place in this new paradigm, for humankind, when freed of a vengeful God, will find itself even more enraptured by the grandeur of the universe, the beauty and mystery of the earth, the awe-inspiring complexity of human emotion. Not through the magico-mythical systems of pre-modern religious ideologies but through the insights of the biological, astronomical, and psychological sciences the human person will be encouraged and enabled to explore the depths of one's own personhood and own social community as well.

Huxley's pleasure at the Bishop's call for a revision of Christianity's portrayal of God is counter balanced by his disappointment at the Bishop's seeming inability to move beyond the dualistic paradigm of traditionalist religion. Bishop Robinson's entrapment in the paradigm precludes any real advance towards an evolutionary religion based on the revelations of "the new dispensation." The Bishop's courage in speaking out is a beginning but for real progress to be made, rational scientifically minded individuals must stand up and pronounce the arrival of the new paradigm, a this-worldliness embracing evolutionary emergence as the core religious experience. The Christian scriptures which rail against the world must be expunged from the experience of the modern person. The Apostle John says, "Love not the world, neither the things that are in the world" (I John 2:15). This mentality resounding from ancient times must now be silenced and a new beckoning must be heeded. Love the earth from whence we came, care for the universe with which we are in partnership, these should be our watchwords says Huxley in his lament at the faltering and then failed start of the good Bishop and those of kindred minds.

*Here we explore Huxley's response to Bishop John A. T. Robinson's book, *Honest to God.*

CHAPTER SEVEN

In The Absence Of God:
The Existentialist Corrective

Before we move further into the thought of Julian Huxley and his dismantling of Biblical religion, it might serve our purposes well to turn for a moment to briefly refresh our memory of the work of Jean-Paul Sartre, a formidable father of existentialism and a major spokesperson for human freedom and human responsibility. Contrary to the proclamations of his detractors, and they are legion within the traditional religious camps, Sartre was never guilty of calling for the human person or the human community to abandon all accountability, all morality, all responsibility as a result of his contention that there is no God. On the contrary and as we shall see, Sartre was a great proponent of human endeavors in the world, requiring maturity and sober judgment, cognizant of the burden of freedom and accountable for irresponsible acts.

Though Sartre was born eighteen years after Huxley, he died five years after Huxley did. So, in some ways, we can assume that their lives somewhat paralleled each other's. What is amazing, even astounding, is that there is no evidence in the lives of either that they were ever aware of each other's life and work. This is astounding because there are so many parallels and amazing because both were so well read and well traveled. Such misses do occur in the history of ideas and we lament the missed potential for great interaction and great influence. We, then, are left with merely our faint efforts at supposing an interaction, imagining a meeting of the minds. And that must suffice.

Sartre, propounding what he has chosen to label "atheistic existentialism," suggests that since "God does not exist … there can be no human nature…" and consequently the "first principle of existentialism" is simply that "Man is nothing else but what he makes of himself -- what is called subjectivity." Furthermore, the challenge of the modern person (called the experience of "forlornness") in the face of the absence of God, is to face all the consequences of this discovery of God's non-existence. Therefore, after God, "Man is the future of man" and is thus "condemned to be free" from the shackles of the Divine. The question of meaning for Sartre is the question of how the human person can live responsibly in a world "after God." Sartre pursues this question ruthlessly in his writings which spanned over sixty years.

Of the modern existentialists, few have had as wide a range of impact through both philosophical and literary writings as has the Frenchman, Jean-Paul Sartre. Consistently inconsistent, Sartre first followed this interest, then that interest, but wherever his thoughts took him, he persisted in his affirmation of the human person. Of those who affected his thought, such as his friends Albert Camus and Maurice

Merleau-Ponty and such giants as Husserl and Heidegger, none had such pervasive impact upon Sartre as did Friedrich Nietszche. In his novel, *La Nausee* (1938) and in a collection of short stories, entitled, *Le Mur* (1939), Sartre lays out in elaborate and stark detail his perception of the predicament of the modern person and society -- the individual, says he, "is without excuse, condemned to freedom, devoid of God." His most notable philosophical work, *L'Etre et la Neant,* 1943 (translated 1956 as *Being and Nothingness*) was and is, without question, a profound piece of rigorous existentialist thought. Had Huxley been more philosophical in his thinking and writing, he certainly would have eventually arrived at this tome of greatness.

The discovery, in Sartre's sense, that "God does not exist" carries with it the necessity for the human person to face responsibly the "consequences" of life "after God." In true existentialist form, Sartre denies that there is a given human nature. That is, human nature as a reality beyond the concept is a non-existent concoction of a philosophy seeking to escape the inevitabilities of a world devoid of Divine Will. Rather, in a world after God, the human community must learn to create for ourselves meaning and purpose, a notion that would have warmed Huxley's heart. The essential character of reality is action, and in action the human person creates values for living from out of the meaninglessness of a godless world. The challenge for humanity is conceived in terms of a creative effort to live responsibly in a world devoid of *a priori* meaning and purpose, i.e., a world discovered and enduring "after God." There is a dialogue which is needed but not provided here between Sartre's sense of meaninglessness as the empowering impetus for persons to become responsible in intentioned action and Huxley's sense of a meaning-system created by the human community with the building blocks of evolutionary science. The question is how to most effectively relate Sartre's notion of life's meaninglessness which is made bearable by intentioned action for the existential betterment of the human community to Huxley's notion of an evolutionary humanism drawing its strength and confidence from scientific knowledge and a sense of purpose and direction derived therefrom.

In a small collection of essays by Sartre, entitled, *Existentialism and Human Emotion*, mentioned above, we have Sartre at his best and briefest. There is, of course, no substitute for reading his *Being and Nothingness* for a comprehensive exposure to his existential and phenomenological system in all its embellished finery. However, in our quest to come to terms with Sartre's understanding of life's meaning alongside that explored and explicated by Huxley's evolutionary humanism, no other collection of his profuse essay-writing equals the one we will consider here.

Of singular excellence is the first essay entitled simply, "Existentialism." It is essentially a defense of Sartre's brand of existentialism "against some charges which have been brought against it." Critics of Sartre have observed that he was at his best in polemical writing and, indeed, this essay corroborates that view. Huxley was not; indeed, he purposely sought to avoid conflict, unlike his grandfather, believing that little is gained in polemic. The charges against existentialism come from a variety of rather diverse camps, especially from the Christians and the communists who have virtually nothing in common save a mutual dislike of Sartre and his philosophical thought. The communists, Sartre was quick to point out with a tinge of amusement, accused him of a multitude of social evils, calling his philosophy "a kind of desperate quietism," "a philosophy of contemplation," "a bourgeois philosophy," and "pure subjectivity." On the other hand, the Christians charge him with inordinately "dwelling on human degradation" and with "pointing up everywhere the sordid, shady, and slimy, and neglecting the gracious and beautiful, the bright side of human nature --- and (with) forgetting the smile of the child." Huxley and Sartre share this in common, namely, that both the Christians and the communists despise their systems of thought, but for very different reasons. Christians abjure Sartre because he points to the dark side of human behavior and disavows the existence of a loving God and Huxley because he points optimistically to a promising future for the earth and humankind precisely in the absence of God. The communists dislike Sartre because he places so much emphasis upon the moral responsibility of the individual with little reference to society whereas they abuse Huxley for believing in an evolutionary process of upward and onward in the absence of a class struggle.

Of course, the charges are wide-ranging and suggestive of deep ideological differences. Nevertheless, with resignation and no little self-confident optimism regarding the outcome of his response, Sartre, unlike the self-effacing Huxley, marches forward "to answer these different charges." From the very beginning, says Sartre, we must understand that by the term "existentialism we mean a doctrine which makes human life possible and, in addition, declares that every truth and every action implies a human setting and a human subjectivity." Sartre refuses to approach the human person from a philosophical anthropology which seeks to discover the nature of humankind. The human person is action and subjectivity. Existentialism begins with the human person in the here and now of the immediate world environment, not in some abstracted Platonic Ideal or religious *imago dei*. Whereas Huxley is eager to see the individual person thrive within the matrix of a social evolution in response to an awareness of the evolutionary processes operative within the universe, Sartre is happy to focus upon the individual person in the immediate experience of existence and, if there is any interest in the social groupings of such persons, it is ancillary and subordinate to the individualized subjectivity of personal being.

Though existentialism "is regarded as something ugly" because it speaks of the "dark side of human life," Sartre is convinced that the real problem is the realization that the human person is, indeed, in a world devoid of supportive illusions. The intimidating and challenging message of existentialism is that "it leaves to man a possibility of choice." Of those who readily decry the "gloomy mood of existentialism," such catch phrases as "it's only human," "we should not struggle against the powers that be," and "we should not resist authority," all too easily foster a mood of resignation. Such a mood constitutes a veritable choice not to choose. Neither Sartre nor Huxley will be contented with a humanity unwilling to assert itself in the face of the inevitabilities of life, whether they be in religious terms or not. There is no God but neither the human person nor the human community has grounds to relinquish responsibility for action, behavior that can better the condition of each individual and society as well. "Who," asks Sartre, "ultimately is more gloomy?" The citizen on the street who systematically opts out of possible choice-making situations because of some childishly assumed cosmic plan or divine scheme, or the existentialist who recognizes that whatever meaning and purpose there is in life is a creation of the human person who chooses to act? The argument is well framed. "Letting go and letting God" is not what Sartre nor Huxley imagine as a responsible address to the human situation.

Though Sartre has defined existentialism with precision, he insists that beyond the definition lies a reality which must be characterized if existentialism is to be significantly and experientially grasped. Sartre derides those flippant culturalists who so vaguely label everything from music and art to scandal and gossip as "existential." "Actually," argues Sartre, "existentialism is the least scandalous, the most austere of doctrines." A task intended strictly for the specialist and philosopher, existentialism is of two kinds. "Christian existentialism" as practiced by Jaspers and Marcel to mention only two among a host, and "atheistic existentialism" such as is done by Heidegger and the French existentialists and not least of whom is Sartre himself. The common bond between these two radically different branches of thought is the belief "that existence precedes essence, or that subjectivity must be the starting point." After God, that is, after the discovery that the world is actually devoid of God, the human person must necessarily become the starting point according to the atheists. Christians say that because of the Incarnation in which God becomes Man, it is with existence rather than essence one must begin to understand the world and our place in it. Huxley and Sartre both agree that the Christians are attempting to have it both ways -- an interventionist power source outside the universe involving himself in the affairs of the world by arbitrarily entering it and leaving it and entering it again according to the whim of circumstances. No such God can be stomached by the existentialism of either the humanists or the atheists. It smacks of cowardice and deception, or "bad faith," as Sartre called it.

In a world conceived theistically, that is, with God as Creator, "the individual man is the realization of a certain concept in the divine intelligence," and this is true whether one likes the theistic philosophical view of Descartes or that of Leibnitz. Though devoid of an ostensibly theistic cosmology, nevertheless, the 18th century did support the "notion that essence precedes existence," and therefore, in Diderot, in Voltaire, and even in Kant, the human person is understood as having a true nature. "This human nature … is found in all men, which means that each man is a particular example of a universal concept, man." Of all the great difficulties resultant from this kind of idealistic metaphysic, a simple one is seen in the difficulty with which Kant had to deal when lumping the "wild-man, the natural man, as well as the bourgeois" into the same human nature. Neither the existentialists nor the humanists will have any part of it. Humanity is defined as action, as behavior, by the choices and decisions we make and not by a predetermined concept of human nature.

The incoherence, or near contradictions, of Christian existentialism becomes apparent when it claims, on the one hand, that existence precedes essence while, on the other, claiming that God is. "Atheistic existentialism," claims Sartre, "is more coherent." In the absence of God, there is still one being in whom existence is first, namely, the human person. Therefore, the existentialist must assert that "there is no human nature, since there is no God to conceive it." Humanity is freed from an *a priori* concept or definition of our being which precedes our actual life-experiences. Human persons now, "after God," are both what we conceive ourselves to be and what we will ourselves to be. We constitute a convergent reality of "conceiving" and "willing," that is, we conceive ourselves to be that which we will ourselves to be. Though Huxley is mute on this fine philosophical point, he would find himself quite comfortable in this discussion in that the human person "takes the initiative" in both self-defining and self-determining who we are and where we are going.

This discovery of the human person's existence devoid of any restricting predefined essence brings with it a profound freedom, but also responsibility. The human person must now "conceive" and "will" itself, or, in terms of the *first principle of existentialism,* "Man is nothing else but what he makes of himself." The human person is a plan which is aware of its own possibilities. This is talk to warm the heart of Huxley for the human person and the human community, indeed, the essential human experience, is at the center of decision making, not some outside force conjured by prayer and imagination, magic and superstition, in hope that the Outside Intervener will fix things. After the demise of a confidence in a Heavenly Plan, a human being comes face to face with one's own subjectivity and immediacy of experience. And, because we exist before we are defined, we are responsible for the definition itself -- what we conceive and will ourselves to be. This is pure evolutionary humanism as Huxley articulated it. "Thus," says Sartre to those who falsely accuse him of moral and social irresponsibility, "existentialism's first move is to make every man aware of what he is and to make the full responsibility of his existence rest on him." No hiding, no escaping, no shirking, no "letting go and letting God" will be tolerated. We are responsible for who we are and what we have done, what we are doing, and what we will do in the future.

This, says Sartre, is the fundamental challenge the existentialist calls forth, namely, the necessity of taking full cognizance of the fact that we alone are responsible for ourselves since God does not exist. The doctrine of the Incarnation is the Christian's final safety net from assuming full responsibility for ourselves and our world. Christians look to a God who has entered from outside in an attempt to offer a corrective to the inside of the universe. The human person has spoiled it all and is now in need of outside assistance. The world does not have within itself the capacity to make things right. It is deficient, it is incomplete without the intervening outside power source. For Huxley and Sartre, this is immaturity raised to the level of an idol. Not only is the human person broken, say the Christians, but the human person cannot fix things back to their unbroken state (pre-Fall) but must await the pleasure of a pathologically irate Creator who destroys a creation gone wrong and then demands the death of his son to appease his rage at the world in order for it to be made right again. This kind of social pathology is in need of psychiatric attention, not obedience, say Sartre and Huxley.

This human subjectivity of which Sartre speaks so admiringly has a dual meaning. First, it means that we choose to make ourselves, and second, we are unable to transcend our own subjectivity. When we choose, we affirm the value of what we have chosen. And furthermore, since every individual chooses, affirms, and values at the same time, that which the individual chooses "is valid for everybody and for our whole age." That is to say, in assuming responsibility for myself in a world after God, I am also choosing for all humanity. "In choosing myself," says Sartre, "I choose the human person," because "my action has involved all humanity." Those who accuse the existentialist of social irresponsibility have failed to understand the profound ethical imperative implicit in this necessity of individuals to "choose man."

Within the context of this imperative to assert

oneself in a world devoid of *a priori* meaning and purpose, that is, a meaning and purpose given prior to the creation of the universe, Sartre says we are better able to understand "what the actual content is" of such characteristic terms of the human condition as anguish, forlornness, and despair. Existentialism considers it unfair of the theists to simply presuppose the existence of a universal essence prior to existence itself. That there is that which is prior to existence baffles the rational mind, the existentialists argue. Better begin with the real, that which is actually in existence at the moment of consciousness, and work from there towards a set of guiding principles rather than to assume that a set of moral mandates have been handed down through the essence of the universe from the magical Creator of all things. There are too many presuppositions in that argument by the theists to attract the scientifically attuned mind of a reflective rational human being. Let's begin with who we are and where we are and work from there. This business of beginning with an essence predetermined by a transcendent power source is an embarrassment to the mature mind according to the humanists and most decidedly the existentialists of the Sartrian hue. Moral behavior and the resulting system of ethics are a cosmic derivative rather than a celestial revelation.

"Man is anguish" say the existentialists. This we must face in all its stark realities. The human person is so because, in a world after God wherein the individual must choose for himself and all humankind, he cannot "escape the feeling of his total and deep responsibility." Here is the imperative, not abandonment of hope and purpose and direction, but, rather, here is the thing which the human person in the absence of a creator God must face, namely, responsibility. Human responsibility is extremely relative and conditional in a world where God exists for, after all, God will eventually fix whatever mess we make of his creation. For the existentialist, no such safety net exists. It is up to us, the human person and the human community, and not some outside source, to address our problems and solve them. And those people among us who disclaim anxiety about the human predicament are simply hiding their anxiety and fleeing it as a coward flees the battle.

This anguish over our condition characterizes all human experience, though it is seldom articulated or dealt with creatively. And though there be those who would seek quietism and passivity in the face of the existential demands to make choices in life, no one can truly escape, for not to choose is, indeed, to choose. Sartre says, for example, that all leaders know of this anguish because, as with all persons, the demands to action necessitate a choice from a number of possibilities, all the while knowing that one's choice "has value only because it is chosen." This intentionality is what brings integrity to the choice. Not that it is given from above, but rather comes from within the human experience rather than from an overseer God. Since there is no *a priori* ethic, that is, no ethical system given prior to existence, human persons create value by virtue of the choices we make in the immediate situation. Ethics is a creative process rather than a responsive one. Anguish is the inevitable result of an awareness that choosing creates value in a world without essential goodness, only existential value.

From Heidegger, Sartre has taken the word "forlornness" and defines it as humanity's realization "that God does not exist and that we have to face all the consequences of this." Sartre is most critical of those secularizing ethicists who liberally profess the need to abolish God yet at minimal expense to society. They would dispose of God but cling to certain values to which they readily attribute *a priori* existence. Thus, social reform movements of a most simplistic sort often say essentially that "nothing will be changed if God does not exist." Sartre will have none of this liberalizing secularism! Everything changes, rather, in a world after God, a world where the human person and the human community is thrown totally upon its own dealings with the world and human life in it. It is a challenge fraught with danger and with promise; but whatever the challenge, it is truly our own challenge, not the challenge of an outside God watching to see how his creation responds. Greek mythology and Biblical religion alike have no place in a mature world of responsible individuals. We are in charge and are likewise charged with the responsibility for every decision and every outcome. The Greeks blamed their gods whereas the peoples of the book, Jews, Muslims, and Christians alike, look to their God for a final answer, for a concluding statement which, according to the humanists of the Sartrian variety, they claim for themselves.

"The existentialist, on the contrary," says Sartre, "thinks it very distressing that God does not exist," primarily because all hope of finding "values in a heaven of ideas" has consequently disappeared. There is no patsy! It is left to us, like it or not. There can no longer be a quest for an *a priori* God, since there is no "infinite and perfect consciousness to think it." Contrary to those liberalizing secularists who speak of a world unchanged by God's absence, Sartre quotes Dostoyevsky in support of atheistic existentialism, who has said: "If God didn't exist, everything would be possible." This, says Sartre, "is the very stating point of existentialism." The experience of forlornness derives from the realization that individuals cannot "start making excuses" for themselves, that in essence, individuals are "condemned to be free." Sartre uses the hard negative of "condemned" rather than "at liberty" owing to the heavy burden freedom carries with it in a world without a God who can be either blamed when things go wrong or blest when things go right. The human person is condemned because we did not create ourselves; yet, we are free because we are responsible for the way we conceive and will ourselves and all others to be. Sartre summarizes this plight and legacy of freedom by saying that "Man is the future of man." Condemnation and freedom go hand in hand -- condemned to life, free to act. "Forlornness and anguish go together" as well, counsels Sartre, for "forlornness implies that we ourselves choose our being and anguish implies an existential awareness of the human condition devoid of *a priori* foundations."

Accompanying forlornness and anguish, despair is the third characteristic of the human situation after the acceptance of being "condemned to freedom" and "free to act." Simply stated, despair, explains Sartre, "means that we shall confine ourselves to reckoning only with what depends upon our will, or on the ensemble of probabilities which make our action possible." Or, in the words of Descartes, "Conquer yourself rather than the world." Human is what we will ourselves to be. Action results from this will, and the moment the possibilities being considered become disassociated from an imperative to action (decision-making and follow-through), Sartre says we must disengage ourselves. We must limit ourselves to what we see, to situations wherein we can act. "Actually," says Sartre, "things will be as man will have decided they are to be." This is profound reliance upon human responsibility and a mandate for moral leadership in a world devoid of a father God who punishes the disobedient and rewards the compliant. The human community, rather than a directive from God, will be what we ourselves choose to be. It is our will, our action, our decision which will make the world what we desire it to be. Could anything be more in keeping with the humanism of Huxley than this?

The result of such a posture is not quietism, but action informed by a will to choose from among various options tempered with the realities of ever-present risk. First, says Sartre, "I should involve myself (and should) act on the old saying, 'Nothing ventured -- nothing gained'." Quietism is a doctrine which lets others do what I think I cannot do or what I fear to do myself. The ethic of existentialism runs diametrically opposite to quietism. An existential ethic declares: "There is no reality except in action," and furthermore, it contends that "Man is nothing else than his plan; he exists only to the extent that he fulfills himself; he is therefore nothing else than the ensemble of his acts, nothing else than his life." We are the sum total of our behavior, our responsibility, our initiative. Sartre has no patience with those who pine for what has not come to pass owing to their own efforts or their own situation. "If only" he considers the ugliest indictment of the human spirit which can be uttered. We have no excuse for there is no God. We must do it ourselves.

Though this view may and does horrify some people, it is really the inevitable result of the discovery of humanity's true situation as being alone in the world. In trying to cope with one's wretchedness, the easy way out is to blame one's condition on circumstances beyond one's control. For those who aspire (without will and action) to greatness, whether in art, literature, music, scholarship or whatever, and fail to realize their wistful dreams, the existentialist offers no comfort. To blame failure on outside circumstances is bad faith, and demonstrably infantile. There is no genius other than that which is manifest and expressed in human effort. "A man is involved in life," says Sartre, "he leaves his impress on it, and outside of that there is nothing." Talk of leaving things in God's hands is simply the abandonment of responsibility by immature individuals fearful of failure. What foolishness to speak of what might have been! If it didn't happen, it wouldn't have happened. There is no "might" to it and "if only" is not allowed. We either make things happen or we don't. "Reality alone is what counts, (for) dreams, expectations, and hopes warrant no more than to define a man as a disappointed dream, as miscarried hopes, as vain expectations." The

107

existentialist will not define the human person in such negative resignation, but rather positively -- "You are nothing else than your life." To label the existentialist pessimistic, then, is to misperceive his true character, viz., which is one of "optimistic toughness." We can do what we will by doing it, not by dreaming it or hoping for it and waiting for it. If we are strong, the future is ours.

Existentialism, rid of restrictive and often times debilitating *a priori* categories of idealistic metaphysics, "defines man in terms of action"; its ethic is an "ethic of action." The existentialist seeks to establish a "doctrine based on truth and not (on) a lot of fine theories full of hope but with no real basis." There is only one real truth, and that is the Cartesian *cogito: I think, therefore, I exist.* There is no universal essence and no universal human nature, but there is undeniably "a universal human condition." This is pure Sartrian philosophy at its most candid and most stark. Though history and geography vary, what does not vary is the necessity for the human person, for all humanity in all times and places "to exist in the world, to be at work there, to be there in the midst of other people, and to be mortal there." By this line of reasoning which says that a single individual experience of whatever sort is analogous to the whole human condition at all times and places, Sartre is led to say that, whether speaking of Chinese, Africans, Indians, or Frenchmen, "every configuration (i.e., experiential situation) has universality in the sense that every configuration can be understood by every man." In this sense, the existentialist can speak of a universality of the human situation and though not given, "it is perpetually being made."

In the arena of the universality of experience, the human person is forced to make choices which affirm human value. No one is exempt from decision-making in a world devoid of God. "In one sense," says Sartre, "choice is possible, but what is not possible is not to choose." And, since the choice is freely made from among a variety of supposedly equally viable possibilities, ethical decisions can be compared to the "making of a work of art." The analogy between ethical choices and aesthetic values is a good one, because with both there is no *a priori,* no pre-established given or pre-set reality. What art and ethics have in common, in a world after God and thus devoid of a heavenly plan, is the qualities of "creation and invention." "Man makes himself," says Sartre, and consequently, both art and ethics are our creation and our invention. There is no God the creator to give it life and form, no God of which we are the image. It is only us in the world. We are left to our own devices to make of the world and our life what we will to make of them. And, reasons Sartre, since "we define man only in relationship to involvement," aesthetics and ethics are possible only as we engage them in our creative and inventive activities. They are not given prior to our own existence, our own acknowledgement of their place in the scheme of things. They gain reality only when we say so and not before.

Recognizing that human depravity must allow for the possibility that some individuals will choose dishonestly, Sartre says that the existentialist is not in a position to pass moral judgment upon dishonest decisions since there are no *a priori* ethical standards. Nevertheless, the existentialist can label dishonesty as error. Dishonesty is a falsehood because it essentially undermines the possibility of "complete freedom of involvement." Just as there is dishonesty in a choice made as if freedom was not absolute, so likewise, Sartre considers as dishonest the position which claims "that certain values exist prior to me..." Complete freedom of involvement implies, even demands, that decisions be made without reliance either upon supposed pre-established ethical categories or upon an intentional limiting of the range of possibilities. Therefore, says Sartre, "the ultimate meaning of the acts of honest men (i.e., those who accept neither universal givens nor arbitrary limitations of possibilities) is the quest for freedom as such."

Honest individuals seek freedom. But freedom for oneself implies freedom for all at the point at which I myself become involved in the pursuit of freedom. That is, as I take freedom as my own personal goal, I do so only by recognizing that I take freedom as the goal of all people. In the context of the recognition of and participation in the "universality of the human situation," the existentialist realizes that the desire for personal freedom is simultaneously a desire for the freedom of all humanity.

Furthermore, and most importantly for the development of an existential ethic, I must face responsibly the realization that as I choose freedom for myself, and thus for all people, I must necessarily pass judgment upon those who for whatever reason choose to hide themselves from the "complete arbitrariness" and the "complete freedom" offered them in their existence. This is true whether they hide by means of allegiance to a supposedly universal code or by means of intentionally narrowing their range of possible choices. Sartre puts his view this way:

> Those who hide their complete freedom from themselves out of a spirit of seriousness or by means of deterministic excuses, I shall call cowards; those who try to show that their existence was necessary, when it is the very contingency of man's appearance on earth, I shall call stinkers.

The content of ethics is relative, says Sartre, but the form of ethics is universal, and that universal is the *human person choosing freedom*. Ethics are mature and responsible to the degree that they seek out and are made in the name of freedom. This notion is explored in historical depth in my book, previously mentioned, *Naturally Good: The Behavioral History of Moral Development (from Charles Darwin to E. W. Wilson)*. And, it must necessarily follow, since values are relative (though their impetus is universal, viz., the human quest for freedom), "values aren't serious, since you choose them." Though, "I'm quite vexed that that's the way it is," says Sartre, nonetheless, he reasons, "if I've discarded God the Father, there has to be someone to invent values." There we have it. In the name of complete freedom of involvement, in a world after God wherein neither cowards nor stinkers have status, the existentialist must come to terms with his anguish, his despair, and his forlornness. This is done by asserting oneself responsibly in the creation

111

and invention of ethical and aesthetical values. "You've got to take things as they come," counsels Sartre.

In this context, Sartre assails a wrong-headed kind of humanism which, as in the cult of mankind propounded by Auguste Comte, for example, "ascribes a value to man on the basis of the highest deeds of certain men." This kind of pseudo-humanism Sartre considers absurd. Another more responsible conception of humanism is exemplified by the existentialist. This kind of existentialistic human reminds human persons that there is no law-maker but ourselves, that we must decide alone, and that our liberation from forlornness will result from our decision not to seek outside of ourselves the goal of freedom. "Existentialism," explains Sartre, "is nothing else than an attempt to draw all the consequences of a coherent atheistic position." With regard to the human necessity of creating values in a world after God, Sartre says by way of concluding this essay:

> Moreover, to say that we invent values means nothing else but this: life has no meaning *a priori* (a prior pre-existent givenness). Before you come alive, life is nothing; it's up to you to give it a meaning, and value is nothing else but the meaning that you choose."

CHAPTER EIGHT

Ethical Humanism and the New Paradigm:
How to Spell "Spiritual Relief"
in a Post-Modern World

"The sense of spiritual relief which comes from rejecting the idea of God as a superhuman being is enormous." These words from Huxley's little classic, *Religion Without Revelation*, have set the tone for this book and state rather clearly from where Huxley and the humanists are coming. It should be clear by now that Huxley and his followers do not imply there is no religion, no spirituality; rather, they simply contend that spirituality and religious consciousness need not have its source and origins from outside the universe, from an intervening transcendent power source. Surely we have demonstrated already that awe, wonder, and reverence are fundamental ingredients in the human experience and need not derive their reality from an afterlife or heaven or a God who stands outside of creation. Religious behavior and spiritual awareness are endemic to the human fabric of our consciousness as they embody our fundamental sense of fascination with the world.

But, for Huxley and the humanists, there is a genuine sense of relief, of a sigh of contentment and respite from anxiety, fear, and pressure from a superhuman personalized God who created the world, destroyed it because of his anger, sent his son demanding that his son die in order to appease his anger, and then threatening everyone with an eternal fire of physical punishment if they did not obey his law even when to determine exactly what that law is seems very problematic. Huxley suggests that the enormity of this sense of relief is not in embracing atheism as a way of living and perceiving but of being exonerated from a primitive notion of a spiritual super being which exercises jurisdiction over the universe and me! Not that we then are at liberty to be merely secular and devoid of any sense of spirituality; on the contrary, this sense of relief is decidedly spiritual in the sense that we are freed and empowered to explore and cultivate our own indigenous spirituality, informed by modern science and mature reason devoid of nursery rhyme superstitions and magical images of a primitive cosmology.

This *natural spirituality*, one might call it, grows out of a liberating consciousness of the demise of the tribal God of supernatural transcendence and grows into the self-reflective awareness of the unity of the cosmos wherein there is no separation of mind and matter, body and spirit, sacred and secular. Rather, there is the realization that, in light of the revelations of evolutionary biology, the universe is a oneness of creation, a unitary reality, a monolithic entity vis a vis the dualism of an archaic theology of divisibility -- God versus humankind, mind versus matter, body versus spirit. To realize and embrace this cosmic discovery that there is no separate supernatural realm but that all phenomena are part and parcel of the same natural process called evolution brings on this "sense of spiritual relief."

Humankind is a central, maybe the central, player in this evolving universe. The biblical God can hardly be a predictable player because, as he is portrayed in biblical mythology, he is sometimes in the world and sometimes out of it, coming and going as whim and fancy move him. Humanity is fully a partner and participant in the evolutionary process, the thinking envelope of the universe and, therefore, responsible for the oversight of its destiny. Reason and rational thought fly in the face of a belief in a supernatural being coming and going, in and out, here and gone, setting rules in a variety of conflicting and contradictory forms and media such that no two groupings of human persons can agree as to exactly what this God has said and to whom and when. Every religion that counts on this intervening power source is set for conflict, suspicion, fear, and, yes, often hatred of other religions who, likewise, believe they have heard or received the words of God, labeling themselves differently from other faith communities. There is no end to the madness once the hypothesis is accepted that this intervening God has in some fashion or another "revealed" his "will" to humankind.

The human community collectively and the human person individually are the key players in the riddle of the universe. A product of three billion years of evolution, it is within the consciousness of the human person that this evolutionary process has become "self-aware." Therefore, whether we like it or not, we are ourselves responsible for the continual evolving of the planet. In spite of this new cosmic consciousness, the human community tends to clutch by-gone systems of comfort in the face of uncertainty. Even when modern science has demonstrated the tribal and superstitious nature of God-centered religion's disenfranchisement from the facts of evolution, we tend to hold on to it as a small child clutches the blanket with which it has slept in hopes that it will continue to offer comfort even when it no longer covers the child from the cold and the uncertainties of daily reality. In the absence or perceived absence of a really viable alternative cosmology and worldview to traditional theism, many times those sensing the void in their lives continue to rearrange the chairs on the Titanic in the full or dim awareness that the ship is going down in spite of all efforts to the contrary.

However, this radical evolutionary crisis of accelerating consciousness through which humankind is presently passing can only be surmounted by an equally radical reorganization of our dominant system of thought and belief. We must move away from the tribalism of a supernatural deity to a scientifically justified awareness of the oneness of the universe and our pivotal role in its on-going development. There is a courage required here, a mature courage of both personal acceptance of the centrality of the evolutionary process in the universe rather than that of our own individual personhood as well as a courage which must assert itself in seeking to foster a pan-psychosocial commitment to the emerging universe. *I am*, therefore, important and *we are* likewise important in cosmic terms, in terms of our indispensable role in the embracing and nurturing of this unitary process within the cosmos.

And there is room, indeed, a necessity, for religion, a religion of the future, a religion constructed out of the materials of this new consciousness and not out of the discarded relics of supernaturalism and dualistic formulations of primitive cosmologies and worldviews. Religion, certainly, is a human construction, a necessarily created ideology which provides answers to life's bafflements, inexorable injustices, and intractable mysteries. Religion functions universally as a mechanism for dealing with the problems and verities of life -- Who are we? Where have we come from? Where are we going? What are we to do? Religion's three-pillared construction consists of (1) an intellectual or ideological framework (called theology), (2) a moral code of behavior (called ethics), and (3) a shared symbolic expression of wonder and awe (called ritual). And religion has been and is forced to either keep stride with socio-cultural and psychological advancements in communal understanding of the answers to these fundamental questions of life or decline in its effectiveness as the "answering mechanism" in the face of bafflement and quandary, exigencies and chaos.

If the Bishop of Woolwich, discussed earlier, is correct in his assessment of the present spiritual character of modern society, then western religion in its three-tiered monotheistic formulation is facing a devolution of viability. Rather, modern science has essentially disenfranchised western religions (Christianity, Judaism, and Islam) from their pre-scientific cosmologies with their accompanying archaic worldviews of supernaturalism and divine interventionism, thus leaving these religious ideologies in a holding position of protectionism and entrenchment. Because these traditional religious systems were constructed during pre-scientific times, their cosmologies and worldviews are out of touch with the common knowledge of historical information available to any school child. "Today," says Huxley, "the God hypothesis has ceased to be scientifically tenable, has lost its explanatory value, and is becoming an intellectual and moral burden to our thought." But, contrary to the misplaced fears of traditionalists, this deep sense of relief brought on by the abandonment of the God-centered universe does not usher in an era of rampant immorality and individual or social irresponsibility. Nevertheless, what must occur is the conscious creation of a cosmology and worldview supported by an ideology, a morality, and a symbolic system worthy of the new consciousness of the oneness of the universe. *We need a religion which matches our science!*

The necessity for this new religion is due fundamentally to the human awareness of and need to respond to the cosmic reality of the divine within nature, what we are calling here "natural religion" (*religio naturalis*) or "natural spirituality" (*spiritualitas naturalis).* The source of this new cosmology and worldview, this evolution-centered rather than god-centered religion, is the universal human sense of "the divine," the very same experiential phenomena which produced tribal religions of the past in the first place. Supernaturalism is not an indispensable ingredient of religion but rather merely an early and naïve human formulation expressive of an awareness of "the stuff of divinity." "The "Gods were," says Huxley, "constructed to interpret man's experiences of this quality," i.e., this stuff of divinity, for the word "divine" does not originally imply the existence of gods but rather testifies to the existence of the experience of the "*mysterium tremendum et fascinans*," the fascinating and tremendous mystery of the meaning and purpose of life infused, as it is, with awe, wonder, and reverence. The gods of old were created to objectify the social experience of both need for authority and source of authority in matters related to the bafflement and inexorable tragedies of life.

The "divine" in human experience, then, may be defined as that which the individual person and human society perceive and define as worthy of adoration, that which elicits awe and wonder. Divinity might be thought of as that raw experiential material of composite experience of individuals and societies out of which religion grows or is created. A humanistic religion, a religion based on the science of evolution and fostered by the awe and wonder perceived and adored in the creation of the cosmos by the human community, invites conscious development as we invite and work to foster ever deepening appreciation of nature and music and art within our offspring. Religion can be grown, developed, fostered, the same way other levels of heightened consciousness can be. It need not be based upon a pre-rationalistic notion of a supernatural being infused with super powers of intervention. A humanistic religion may very well be intentionally grown from the materials of mathematics, biology and psychology instilled with the wonder, awe, and reverence induced from a genuine encounter with scientific knowledge and the created world.

By embracing evolutionary biology as the source of all things, this humanistic religion can proceed with the fundamental hypothesis of growth and development, fulfillment and achievement, as the purpose and direction of its function within society and for each individual. Because human potentialities constitute the world's greatest resource, as yet only barely grasped, then by tapping and directing these vast resources of human possibility, the religion of the future has at its disposal the full participation of the consciousness of the universe, human consciousness, in pursuit of ever greater senses of personal and social fulfillment and achievement. The resulting moral codes and symbolic rituals will necessarily have to be created out of the combined energy and experience of those involved in developing the ideological framework of this *humanistic religion of evolutionary consciousness.*

For example, in place of any notion of personal eternity, this effort will direct itself to a sense of enduring process. A sense of personal salvation will be replaced with the notion of a continuing development of a deepening sense of commitment to and responsibility for the physical environment of the world and the psychological environment of the human personality. Salvation will then mean an investment by the human community in the perpetuity of the world rather than a personally enduring self. Salvation may imply survival but not personally but cosmically. The Christian's casual disregard for the longevity of the world's existence owing to a fundamental belief that when Jesus returns the world will be destroyed (thus implying that God himself has only a passing interest in the earth itself), the humanist is unequivocally committed to the perpetual endurance of the world for its own sake and the sake of all life here on it. This is pure Julian Huxley here and the message is clear and sound. No petitionary prayers to a supernatural and intervening being, an external power source, will be thought relevant or rational, but adoration and aspiration will characterize the self-reflective meditations of the human person and society at large. Thru self-examination and socially tutored psychological exploration, individuals and societies will identify and foster mechanisms, for deepening senses of responsibility and fulfillment.

POSTSCRIPT

Why Bother?

Of course, the more jaded and crusty secular humanists among us marvel at the bother. It might be argued, and somewhat persuasively, that the bother is not worth the results for the humanists already know what they know and the religious community is certain of its position. It certainly could be argued, as was said early in this discussion, that "all argumentation with presupposition is circular," and, thus, the humanists end where they started and likewise do the faithful. To employ traditionally sacrosanct nomenclature such as "religion," "God," "Divinity," "awe," "reverence," "wonder," and the like while providing each one with a somewhat different meaning not only does not move dialogue ahead but seems dangerously close to actually contributing to its ineffectiveness. If we can't agree on the meaning of the words we use, then how can we ever come to an understanding, to say nothing of an agreement, on these issues?

Still and all, the warm-blooded humanists who so desperately desire to free religiously trapped persons from their shackles can hardly resist proposing the use of the old language with new meaning, or, more precisely, with a deeper and more reflective understanding of our present reality. For those who experience deeply awe, wonder, and reverence in the world about them, in themselves, and in their encounters with others, the yearning for a validation of that experience is real and legitimate. Yet, many of these same individuals find themselves disenfranchised from the religious establishment for refusing to embrace a pre-modern notion of an interventionist God, a God of the Bible, who consistently exhibits primitive and irrational behavior. The Garden of Eden, the flood, parting of water and stopping the sun, blood sacrifice of the son to appease the anger of the father God, the virgin birth of a God/Man, an eternal damnation by fire -- all of these things fly in the face of reason and modern science. However, the experience of awe, wonder, and reverence still persist, even grow, in the midst of a deepening understanding of the evolutionary process of creation. Isn't there a legitimate place for such as these in the world?

REFERENCES

Huxley's bibliography

Essays of a Biologist (1923)
Animal Biology (1927), *with J. B.S. Haldane*
Religion Without Revelation (1927)
The Science of Life (1923), with *H. G. Wells*
*Scientific Research and Social Needs (*1934)
*We Europeans (*1936), with *A. C. Haddon*
The Living Thoughts of Darwin (1939)
The New Systematic (1940)
Evolution: The Modern Synthesis (1942)
*Evolutionary Ethics (*1943)
Touchstone for Ethics (1947)
*Man in the Modern World (*1947)
Heredity, East and West (1949)
Biological Aspects of Cancer (1957)
Towards a New Humanism (1957)
New Bottles for New Wine (1958)
Knowledge, Morality, and Destiny (1959)
*The Humanist Frame (*1962)
*Essays of a Humanist (*1964)
Evolutionary Humanism (1964)
*From an Antique Land (*1966)
*The Courtship Habits of the Great Grebe (*1968)
Memories (1971 - 73), *2 Volumes*

John H. Morgan

Huxley Sources Used in This Study

Religion Without Revelation
Knowledge, Morality, and Destiny
Julian Huxley: Scientist and World Citizen (1887-1975)
UNESCO
Julian Huxley: Memories
Evolutionary Humanism

Secondary Sources Consulted

The Huxleys by Ronald W. Clark

Pat Duffy Hutcheon, "Julian Huxley: From materialism to Evolutionary Naturalism," *Humanist in Canada*, Autumn, 1999.

Timothy J. Madigan, "Evolutionary Humanism Revisited: The Continuing Relevance of Julian Huxley," American Humanist Association, 2002.

"Is Secular Humanism a Religion?," in Roger Eastman's *The Way of Religion* (NY: Harper & row, 1975), Chapter 12, entitled, "Humanism: Man Is the Measure."

John H. Morgan, "Ethical Humanism and the 'New Divinity': Exploring Post-Biblical Religion In a Secular World, or How to Spell 'Spiritual Relief'," delivered at the 2006 Oxford University Summer Programme in Theology.

John H. Morgan, *Naturally Good: The Behavioral History of Moral Development (from Charles Darwin to E. O. Wilson),* South Bend, IN: Cloverdale Books, 2005.

John H. Morgan, *Being Human: Perspectives in Meaning and Interpretation (Essays in Religion, Culture, and Personality) Second Edition,* South Bend, IN: Quill Books, 2006.

ABOUT THE AUTHOR

John H. Morgan, Ph.D. (Hartford), D.Sc. (C.A.S./London), Psy.D. (Foundation House/ Oxford), is The Karl Mannheim Professor of the History and Philosophy of Social Sciences at the Graduate Theological Foundation where he has also been President since 1982. Since 1998, he has been teaching in the international summer program of Oxford University where he was appointed to the program's Board of Studies in 1995. He has held postdoctoral appointments at Harvard, Yale, and Princeton and has been a National Science Foundation Science Faculty Fellow at the University of Notre Dame and has also held three postdoctoral appointments at the University of Chicago. He also holds a joint faculty appointment at Cloverdale College as The Sir Julian Huxley Professor of the History and Philosophy of Education. The author of over thirty books and scores of scholarly articles, his latest books include *Being Human: Perspectives in Meaning and Interpretation (Essays in Religion, Culture, and Personality)*, 2003; *The P.R.I.M.E. Factor: A Radical Philosophy of Collaborative Education*, 2004; and *Naturally Good: The Behavioral History of Moral Development (from Charles Darwin to E. O. Wilson)*, 2005.